A Journey to Self-Worth

NIKKI HARDEN

Chosen and Enough

Trilogy Christian Publishers
A Wholly Owned Subsidiary of Trinity Broadcasting Network
2442 Michelle Drive, Tustin, CA 92780

Copyright © 2024 by Nikki Harden

Scripture quotations marked (KJV) taken from The Holy Bible, King James Version. Cambridge Edition: 1769.

Scripture quotations marked niv are taken from the Holy Bible, New International Version®, NIV®. Copyright © 1973, 1978, 1984, 2011 by Biblica, Inc.™ Used by permission of Zondervan. All rights reserved worldwide. www.zondervan.com. The "NIV" and "New International Version" are trademarks registered in the United States Patent and Trademark Office by Biblica, Inc.™

Scripture quotations marked nkjv are taken from the New King James Version®. Copyright © 1982 by Thomas Nelson. Used by permission. All rights reserved.

All rights reserved, including the right to reproduce this book or portions thereof in any form whatsoever. For information, address Trilogy Christian Publishing Rights Department, 2442 Michelle Drive, Tustin, CA 92780.

Trilogy Christian Publishing/ TBN and colophon are trademarks of Trinity Broadcasting Network.

For information about special discounts for bulk purchases, please contact Trilogy Christian Publishing.

Trilogy Disclaimer: The views and content expressed in this book are those of the author and may not necessarily reflect the views and doctrine of Trilogy Christian Publishing or the Trinity Broadcasting Network.

10 9 8 7 6 5 4 3 2 1
Library of Congress Cataloging-in-Publication Data is available.

ISBN 979-8-89333-412-8
ISBN (ebook) 979-8-89333-413-5

Contents

Dedication 5
Privacy Notice 7
Introduction 9

Chapter 1: *The Unexpected Shift (Part 1)* 13
Chapter 2: *The Unexpected Shift (Part 2)* 19
Chapter 3: *The Journey Begins* 23
Chapter 4: *The Defining Stage* 27
Chapter 5: *The Mind Transformation Stage* 33
Chapter 6: *It's Behind Me Now* 41
Chapter 7: *Rejected, But He Accepted Me* 49

Congratulations! 57

Chapter 8: *Sufficiently Chosen* 59
Chapter 9: *His Beloved* 63
Chapter 10: *Embracing Your Style* 69
Chapter 11: *Be Unapologetically You* 77

Acknowledgments 85

Dedication

This book is dedicated to the One who saw beyond my faults and shortcomings, who chose me even when I felt unworthy and inadequate. I am forever grateful for Your unfailing love, mercy, and grace, which have sustained me through life's toughest challenges.

Your call and blessings are a testament to Your faithfulness and goodness, and I am honored to share my story with others. Through the pages of this book, I hope to inspire others to seek You with all their hearts and to experience the same joy and hope that I have found in Your love.

Thank You for choosing me and for never giving up on me. I am forever in Your debt, Abba.

Signed,
the one you chose

Privacy Notice

To ensure that the identities of my beloved family and friends remain protected and secure, I have taken the responsible step of changing their names in this book.

I understand that privacy is a fundamental right and take it seriously. I intend to preserve the anonymity of my loved ones and respect their wishes for confidentiality. Their trust and support have been instrumental in bringing this book to fruition, and I am deeply grateful to them for allowing me to share my story.

Introduction

Have you ever experienced that gnawing sense of inadequacy, the feeling that you're not bright, pretty, or bold enough? Or, worse still, you questioned your worthiness for the blessings God has given you? We have all been there, pondering questions like "Who am I?" "Where do I belong?" and "What is my purpose?" The journey of self-discovery is marked by profound questions that echo through the recesses of our minds, seeking elusive answers.

I've struggled with these questions, facing unworthiness and self-doubt. Rejections and abandonment issues became unwelcome companions, casting a shadow on my relationships, ministry, and even professional endeavors. It was as if Satan took every chance to remind me of my flaws, attempting to strip away the God-given confidence within, leaving me in a state of blindness to my true identity (Psalm 139:14 NIV – "I am fearfully and wonderfully made").

However, in life, there comes a point when the weariness of being entangled in these lies becomes unbearable. I reached that point, tired of the devil's narrative conflicting with the reality of God's blessings in my life. Turning to God, I found comfort in His words, realizing the need to break free from the chains of falsehoods that bound me. It was a journey of discovering who I truly am in Him, rooted in His perfect love and captivated by His truth.

The desire to be seen and chosen for who we are is universal. Yet, believing that someone can see through the filters we present to the world can be a daunting challenge — a recent encounter after moderating a conference brought this to light for me. A young lady approached, moved by the impact of God's work through me, and asked a powerful question: "Who are you? By now, we should have known who you are." It was a moment of soul searching, torn between presenting the strong woman of God and acknowledging the scars of rejection.

My journey, marked by challenges, summarizes the paradox of being chosen by God while wrestling with feelings of unworthiness. Trauma, grief, and the relentless whispers of the enemy led me to question the divine choice. The rerun of inadequacy played continuously, attempting to obscure the truth of God's purpose.

So, how do I respond to the young lady's question? Who are you? I am a woman of God who has weathered challenges but is unwavering in my trust in His plan — a servant committed to positively impacting and navigating a gritty and grace-filled path.

I found comfort in God's healing embrace and guidance in pursuing self-worth. I sought the key to unlocking my true identity by deeply exploring His Word. His grace and mercy transformed my perception, revealing a self no longer defined by past struggles but aligned with His intended purpose.

This book is not just another recounting of experience but an invitation for you to join me on a journey intended to help, inspire, encourage, and impact those battling rejection, abandonment, inadequacy, and low self-worth by offering practical strategies to overcome these obstacles. It is a narrative born from personal experiences, a testimony to the transformative power of embracing one's true identity given by God. It is a vessel of inspiration, encouragement, and empowerment.

As you embark on this voyage alongside me, I hope my story resonates with your struggles, guiding you to realize your immeasurable value and untapped God-given potential. As you navigate these pages, you will find transparency and honesty, acknowledging triumphs and challenges. Exercises and prompts await, guiding you toward recognizing negative patterns and cultivating positive habits.

May this narrative resonate with your struggles and guide you toward self-discovery. By the journey's end, I aspire for you to feel inspired and equipped with the tools to embrace your true self. You are loved, chosen, and enough; may this book remind you of that undeniable truth.

CHAPTER 1
The Unexpected Shift (Part 1)

Once the storm is over, you will not remember how you made it through or how you managed to survive. You will not even be sure, in fact, whether the storm is really over. But one thing is certain: when you come out of the storm, you will not be the same person who walked in.

— Haruki Murakami

As humans, we often approach life with a sense of control and direction, mapping out our futures with the best intentions. We plan for the good times and the bad, confident that we can handle whatever life throws our way. However, the reality is that life is unpredictable and ever-changing, and no matter how carefully we plan, there will always be unexpected twists and turns along the way.

Life can be unpredictable and full of changes, some of which can significantly impact us. Unfortunately, we are not typically taught how to deal with these changes in school or elsewhere, leaving us struggling to cope with the overwhelming emotions and confusion they can bring. We may experience loss and not know who we are or our purpose. When unprepared, it can feel like the very foundation of our lives is crumbling, leaving us uncertain about the future.

I have personally experienced this feeling of confusion and pain when I went through significant changes in my life. No one could have prepared me for the impact of these changes, leaving me questioning everything, including my identity and self-worth. I was left feeling lost, alone, and in pain. Looking back, I wish someone had taught me how to prepare myself for these changes and to cope with the emotions that came with them.

I am the youngest girl of five siblings, with three beautiful older sisters and one handsome older brother, all from my mother's side. We were remarkably close (though we have had our share of difficulties, we are still close to this day), and our mother was the glue that held us together. A devoted deaconess, she loved God wholeheartedly and always put her children first, embracing everyone else's children as her own.

One day, returning home from school, I found my sister Lanette in my bedroom, visibly distraught. Sensing something was wrong, I knew trouble was brewing. Later, Lanette gathered us outside to share the devastating news: our mother was seriously ill, with bleak prospects for recovery. Tears flowed as we vowed to remain strong for her.

In the ensuing weeks, the fear of losing my mother weighed heavily on my heart. I wrestled with the uncertainty of where to turn for love and understanding in her absence.

Amidst my mother's declining health, a Friday night trip turned perilous. I had planned to ride with my boss from work that night, but my sister Laya and her friend Kennedy offered me a ride instead. As I exited the car, Kennedy's playful antics caused her to accidentally strike me with the vehicle three times, leaving me trapped underneath. In a moment, I saw my life flash before my eyes. By God's grace, I could escape from beneath the car when it finally stopped. They rushed me to the hospital, where subsequent examinations revealed I had sustained fractures in my pelvic bone and dislocations in both hip bones. Throughout my hospital stay, as I wrestled with my injuries, my mother's health declined simultaneously in another medical facility. Helpless and unable to walk, I was bound to a wheelchair and the confines of a hospital bed. With my family preoccupied with my mother's condition, my young mind struggled with confusion and loneliness. Yet, in my despair, I turned to God, recognizing His presence and seeking solace amidst the chaos. Though unable to fully comprehend the gravity of the calling upon my life, I found guidance and strength through His teachings, learning the essence of faith and its application during trying times.

The day I returned home from the hospital, eager to see my mother, a foreboding overwhelmed me. That night, an unshakable intuition hinted at her passing. Despite dismissing it as imagination, the somber expressions of my aunt and grandmother confirmed my worst fears: my mother was gone. I hadn't even had the chance to bid her farewell, left only to see her in a casket while I was constricted to a wheelchair. The realization brought immense sorrow yet a sense of relief, knowing she was no longer suffering.

As I grappled with my mother's death and my physical limitations, I found myself questioning my identity and place in the world. Feelings I had suppressed in my childhood are now staring me in the face. Who was I without my mother's love and guidance? How could I rebuild my life when everything was falling apart? These questions weighed heavily on my mind, and I struggled to find answers.

Despite the despair and loneliness, I refused to give up hope. With each passing day, I found strength in my mother's memories and my faith's unwavering support. I drew upon the lessons she had taught me about resilience and perseverance, knowing she would want me to keep fighting, even in the darkest times.

Slowly but surely, I began to rebuild my life. With God's divine intervention and the unwavering encouragement of loved ones, I took small steps forward, literally and figuratively. I learned to walk again, not just in a physical sense but also in terms of reclaiming my sense of self and purpose.

Through this journey of loss and recovery, I discovered a newfound sense of resilience within myself. I realized that adversity does not define us but shapes us into the people we are meant to be. It was a journey of self-discovery and growth, filled with challenges and triumphs.

I emerged more robust and more resilient than I ever thought possible. I may have lost my mother and broken a few bones in the process, but her love and guidance continue to inspire me every day. And while the road ahead may be uncertain, I face it with courage and determination, knowing I can conquer whatever obstacles come my way.

Reflecting on my journey, I am reminded of embracing life's unpredictability and finding strength in adversity. Through our struggles, we discover our true resilience and emerge stronger than we ever thought possible.

CHAPTER 2

The Unexpected Shift (Part 2)

Life is an expedition marked by moments of triumph and joy and periods of profound sadness and loss. Amidst the ebb and flow, it's easy to lose sight of the light that shines within us. Yet, it's during these darkest moments that our true strength is unveiled.

In the previous chapter, I revealed a significant transformation that I underwent, both physically and emotionally. This transformation left me questioning whether God had made a mistake in choosing me. I had lost my sense of identity and belonging, and without my mother to validate my existence, I felt adrift.

Adding insult to injury, the accident that I had during that time resulted in me missing my last semester of eleventh-grade credits. I had to work hard to make up for lost time while earning all my 12th-grade credits. It felt like one obstacle after another, but I refused to give in. At only 17 years old, I had to work and go to school simultaneously, and my faith was tested. I had to cry in private because people were watching, hoping to see me fail without my mother's support.

During the long, lonely nights in the hospital, the actual depth of my resilience became evident. In the silence of my pain, comfort found me through prayer, and I drew strength from the unshakeable belief that I was never alone. Each passing day taught me to lean into discomfort, embrace uncertainty, and trust the journey's wisdom.

I understand that many of us experience life-changing situations that can leave us feeling lost and questioning our values, purpose, and career choices. Even if your story differs from mine, you may face similar challenges that leave you feeling inadequate, overwhelmed, and unprepared. It is natural to blame ourselves when life throws us a curveball, but we must accept that we cannot always control how things happen. Instead, we should embrace the process, understand that we are not alone in our struggles, and appreciate the lessons we learn.

As I write this, I am reminded of Isaiah 43:18-19 NKJV, where the Lord encourages us to let go of the past and focus on the present and the future. The scripture reads: "Do not remember the former things, nor consider the things of old. Behold, I am doing a new thing. Now it shall spring forth; shall you not know it? I will make a road in the wilderness and rivers in the desert." Although we may not fully comprehend why we endured the trials and tribulations we faced or what purpose they serve in our lives, we must remember that God has a plan for everything. We should acknowledge that the challenges we face not only strip away the things we are holding onto but also shape and mold us into the kind of person we were meant to be. It is an ongoing process, but with faith and patience, we can learn to navigate life's challenges and become stronger and wiser on the other side.

Although I felt unworthy and faced insecurities, through tears, laughter, doubts, and clarity, I embraced my worthiness. I accepted myself, flaws and all, recognizing that my value wasn't contingent upon external validation. It was a radical act of self-love — a conscious choice to honor the unique essence that defines me.

Along this winding path, we encounter obstacles — moments of uncertainty and setbacks — but each challenge unveils reservoirs of strength within us. Each hurdle becomes an opportunity for growth, a chance to unearth dormant potential.

Delving deeper into our souls, we will uncover hidden treasures — dreams, gifts, and truths waiting to be embraced. Our past does not define us, and trials don't diminish our worth. We are a canvas awaiting vibrant colors of possibility, a curtain of resilience woven with threads of courage and grace.

Standing on the cliff of our potential, we will feel empowered, recognizing that the most extraordinary adventure lies in the journey itself — a journey of self-discovery, embracing the beautiful complexity of being human, and dancing to the rhythm of our heartbeat.

We must embrace this journey with open arms, trusting in the wisdom of our hearts and believing in our limitless potential. Though the road ahead may twist and turn, remember that we are the author of our story — the architect of our destiny.

I encourage you not to shrink from challenges or tremble in uncertainty. Within you lies the strength of a thousand warriors, the courage of a lionheart, and the resilience of the ages. You are more powerful, beautiful, and worthy than you dare to believe.

When doubt knocks, stand firm in knowing you are enough — your worthiness is inherent, and your potential limitless. You are not just a chapter in the book of life but the author of your destiny. Rewrite the script, chart a course that defies convention, and create a unique narrative.

The journey awaits. Are you prepared to board the ship on the adventure of a lifetime to discover the boundless beauty of your soul?

CHAPTER 3

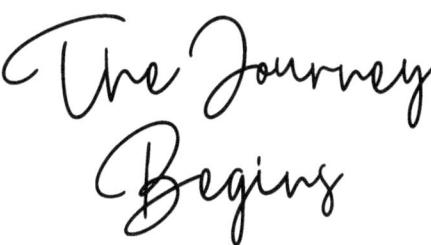
The Journey Begins

A journey of a thousand miles begins with a single step.

— Lao Tzu

Trauma and life-changing movements can be immobilizing and stop us from seeing ourselves the way we were created to be. It can come in the form of grief, abuse, or abandonment; the pain can be unbearable. It can leave us feeling powerless, struggling to know where to begin the process of healing and rebuilding our self-worth. Despite what others might think, the pain can linger, making it difficult to move forward. But it's not impossible.

Lao Tzu, a prominent Chinese philosopher and founder of Taoism, once said that every journey, no matter how long or daunting, starts with a single step. This quote has a deep meaning and can be empowering, especially during challenging times. It reminds us that no matter the obstacle, we can overcome it by taking the first step.

The power of this quote lies in its encouragement to be courageous, to act, and have faith in ourselves. We all face challenges and setbacks in life, and it can be easy to feel lost or overwhelmed. However, by taking the first step, we bring ourselves closer to healing and our purpose and begin gaining the momentum to keep going.

It was daunting to relearn how to walk again. There were times when I was in the hospital wondering if I would be able to walk again because it seemed impossible. I had to start from scratch and teach my body this essential task. Getting back on my feet took a lot of effort, patience, and perseverance. Every step was painful, but I kept going. I started walking with a limp, but the more I kept at it, the more my legs began performing the way they were meant to.

Like how we acquire the skill of walking, we also need to develop the ability to handle the challenges that life throws us. Just as we take our first steps with unsteady legs, we stumble through life until we gain enough experience and understanding to navigate it more confidently and efficiently.

To achieve healing and self-acceptance, we must first acknowledge and accept our current situation, along with the pain and emotional turmoil that often accompanies any traumatic or sudden change in our lives that causes us to struggle with our identity. We commonly avoid the pain and discomfort of these difficult situations and act as though expressing vulnerability or uncertainty is a sign of weakness. However, true strength often lies in surrendering to our emotions and accepting them for what they are. Only then can we move forward and work towards a brighter future.

In the Bible, in 2 Corinthians 12:9-10, the Apostle Paul speaks about a "thorn in his flesh." He believed that this thorn was a messenger of Satan, which was causing him a lot of frustration and pain. He prayed three times to have it removed, but the Lord told him that His grace was sufficient for him and that his strength is made perfect in weakness.

After hearing this, Paul accepted the Lord's response and boasted in his infirmities, knowing that the power of Christ would rest upon him. He found pleasure in his infirmities, persecution, and distress for the sake of Christ. He said, "For when I am weak, then I am strong."

Paul understood that when he embraced his weakness and acknowledged his struggles, he found the strength to move forward. He realized that his pain was not a sign of weakness but an opportunity for God's strength to shine through him. In this way, he found joy in his challenges and suffering, understanding that they were a necessary part of his spiritual growth.

It is a powerful reminder that when we try to escape pain, we delay the healing process and the transformation it will bring to our lives. Instead, when we embrace our struggles and allow God to work through us, we can find strength and joy amid our challenges.

During a period of recovery, I was confronted with a range of complex emotions, such as sorrow, rejection, and an identity crisis. Initially, these challenges appeared impossible, and I felt I was losing control. However, I resolved not to let them take hold of me. Instead, I was determined to use these obstacles as an opportunity for growth and self-discovery. Through this process, I understood that life's challenges are not meant to expose our weaknesses but to bring out our innate strength and resilience.

I'm still on my journey of self-discovery, which has not always been easy but undoubtedly worthwhile. I discovered that sometimes, we must be both the messenger and the message. Our experiences can inspire and motivate others to persevere through their difficulties. Through these struggles, I also learned to embrace my strengths and share my story with others, hoping that it could help them find their path to healing and self-discovery.

If you are struggling to find your way through your pain, please know that you have the power within you to start your journey toward healing and self-worth. At first, it might seem daunting, but taking the first step is crucial, and everything else will follow. It would help if you took the time to reflect on your thoughts and feelings and seek help if needed. Therapy is frowned upon, but it can be very beneficial, or talking to a trusted friend, mentor, or pastor can also help. You can and should seek guidance from God through prayer.

Remember that healing is a procedure that requires patience, resilience, and self-compassion. It is essential to own your pain and allow yourself time to heal. At the same time, acting toward your healing journey is equally important, one step at a time. Don't hesitate to use the power of this quote and start your journey today towards a brighter tomorrow. Remember that with time, patience, and continuous effort, you can prevail over any hurdle and achieve the life that God predestined you to have.

CHAPTER 4

The Defining Stage

The Bible recounts the story of the Children of Israel, who were enslaved in Egypt for 400 years. The Lord had allowed them to become servants in Egypt, but after four centuries, He heard their cries for help and sent Moses to lead them out of Egypt. However, Moses was initially unsure about his ability to speak well enough to convince Pharaoh to release the Israelites. Despite his doubts, with the help of God, he eventually succeeded.

God sent ten plagues upon Egypt, with the final one being the death of the firstborn, including the heir to the throne of Pharaoh. After this, Pharaoh finally let the Israelites go, but his heart was still hardened. He and his army went after them, but after Moses parted the Red Sea with God's help, the children of Israel crossed safely, while the waters wiped out Pharaoh and his entire army.

Then, Moses led Israel into the wilderness, where they wandered for forty years. In the wilderness, the children of Israel fought against Moses and God the whole time. They complained and said they would rather be servants in Egypt than be in the wilderness, where they had to trust the unknown. During their time in the wilderness, they were called to shed their old selves and embrace the unknown. They were forced to reckon with who they were and who they wanted to become.

The wilderness is often described as the defining stage of life, where we are confronted with our deepest fears, limitations, and authentic selves. In this uncharted territory, we are called to uncover our hidden strengths and weaknesses and discover the path leading us to our true purpose. The defining stage of life is where our past, present, and future converge, and we are forced to reckon with who we are and who we want to become.

As we define our lives, we encounter various layers we need to peel off. These layers could be our fears, unforgiveness, insecurities, doubts, or anything that holds us back from realizing our true potential. In the upcoming chapters, I will dig deeper into these layers and help you understand how to shed them fully and embrace yourself. This process of self-discovery will enable you to pursue your purpose with passion and strength, unrestrained by past traumas or limiting beliefs.

Tracing the Roots

The previous chapter offered valuable insight into taking that first step on any journey. It emphasized the significance of pausing to reflect on our present state. This requires us to confront the pain and acknowledge its effects on us. We can only move forward with a clear sense of direction and purpose. Once we have recognized our pain, we must deal with it. We need to break up and understand what caused us to experience self-doubt. We must ask ourselves why we feel inadequate for a particular job, ministry assignment, relationship, or love. This contemplation allows us to identify the root cause of our insecurities. Doing so makes us better equipped to overcome them and achieve our goals.

In the last chapter, we learned the significance of acknowledging our pain and its underlying causes. This enables us to take charge of our lives and confidently move forward. The analogy of retracing our steps when we lose something and can't find it is particularly relevant in this context. Just as we mentally go through every place we've been and revisit each spot physically to recover what we've lost, we need to rethink our past experiences to understand how they have shaped our current state of mind.

To do this, we must plow into our past and identify the people and experiences that have caused us pain and left us unsure of ourselves. This requires us to be reflective and honest with ourselves as we explore the memories and emotions buried deep within us. By doing so, we can identify the negative beliefs and thinking patterns holding us back and preventing us from achieving our full potential.

To explore our emotions and psyche, we must ask tough questions that often go unasked. For instance,

- At what point did you begin to feel like you were not measuring up?
- What person or experience caused this pain and discomfort within you?

- In what ways has this feeling molded your personality, relationships, decisions, beliefs, and goals?

By exploring these questions, we can better understand ourselves and our experiences and work towards greater self-awareness and personal growth.

It is important to note that this process may not be easy or comfortable. We may uncover painful memories and emotions we have suppressed for years. However, we can only begin to heal and move forward by facing these uncomfortable truths. By addressing each pain point, layer by layer, we can gradually free ourselves from the shackles of self-doubt and negative self-talk.

Tracing the roots of our negative emotions is a journey that requires courage, honesty, and self-compassion. It is not a quick fix but a gradual process of self-discovery and healing. However, by taking the time to understand our past experiences, we can emerge more robust, faster to recover, and better equipped to face whatever challenges life throws our way.

During a period of self-reflection, I found myself delving into the root of my problems and the defining moment that led to them. One of the critical issues I discovered was my struggle with self-worth and how it had held me back from achieving my goals. Looking back on my life, I couldn't help but wonder where my feelings of rejection came from and when they began. Was it due to my aunts and grandmother, who had always told me that I was incapable of accomplishing anything and had instilled negativity in my mind? Despite their love for me, their comments had a lasting impact, causing me to question my abilities and self-worth. Or was it because of my siblings, who had always seemed to dislike me no matter what I did? I had tried to fit in with them by copying their behavior, but it never felt authentic, and I felt like an imposter.

As I reflect upon my past experiences, I realize that losing my mother was not the only reason I felt rejected and inadequate. My father's broken promises also contributed significantly to my emotional turmoil. My father often made grand promises to me in my childhood but never kept them. His inability to follow through with his commitments left me feeling heartbroken and disappointed. I still vividly remember how he would promise to spend time with us, but he would never show up, making me feel insignificant. When I finally met my father for the first time at fourteen, I was hopeful and excited, thinking our relationship would improve. However, my mother passed away from being in the hospital soon after, and my father failed to be there for me when I needed him the most. His absence caused me to feel even more rejected and unworthy of his love and support.

Reflecting on this realization, I began to understand how these negative comments, actions, and experiences had impacted my self-worth and self-belief. Although it was a complex process, I knew I had to confront these issues one layer at a time to move forward and achieve my goals. As I did so, I started to see myself in a new light and began to believe that I could accomplish anything I set my mind to. I learned that it was crucial to surround myself with people who supported and encouraged me rather than those who brought me down.

The "wilderness" stage of life is a period of transition that we all go through. It's when we leave behind the familiar and venture into the unknown, facing uncertainty, confusion, and a sense of loss. During this stage, we encounter challenges and difficulties that we may not have experienced before. However, it's essential to understand that this stage is not one to be rushed, as it plays a critical role in shaping our lives. The wilderness stage is a time of transformation, where we can discover who we are and what we want from life. It's an opportunity for growth, self-discovery, and personal development.

Just like the children of Israel who journeyed through the wilderness to reach God's promised land, we, too, must travel through this stage to reach our desired destination. It may be a difficult journey, but it's also a time for learning and exploration. We can learn valuable lessons from our experiences in the wilderness and discover our passions, interests, and purpose in life. We can develop resilience and better understand ourselves by embracing this period and not rushing through it. We can take the time to reflect on our lives and experiences and learn from them. This will help us grow and become the best version of ourselves.

Therefore, we must take the time to go through this process and not rush it. We should look at the world with a curious and open mind and learn from our experiences. Can we honestly say we know who we are and what we want from life? The wilderness stage of life may be challenging, but it's also an opportunity for personal growth and self-discovery.

CHAPTER 5

The Mind Transformation Stage

And be not conformed to this world: but be ye transformed by the renewing of your mind, that ye may prove the good and acceptable and perfect will of God.

— Romans 12:2 (KJV)

The mind is an incredibly complex and sophisticated tool that allows us to think, reason, and make sense of the world. It is the driving force behind all our actions and decisions; without it, we would be unable to function as intelligent beings. The mind constantly processes information, analyzes patterns, and makes predictions to help us navigate the complexities of life. It is a remarkable tool that is both a blessing and a responsibility.

A person's memory is a complex process that involves three different stages: sensory memory, short-term memory, and long-term memory. Sensory memory is responsible for registering and storing sensory experiences such as sights, sounds, and tastes we encounter daily. However, this type of memory is fleeting and lasts only a few seconds before it fades away. Short-term memory, or working memory, is responsible for holding information for a short period. It receives information from sensory memory and processes it before sending it to long-term memory. Long-term memory, on the other hand, oversees storing information for extended periods, from minutes to years. This type of memory is like a library where data is stored for later retrieval. You can think of it like the files and documents on your computer screen. If you want to keep them, save them on your computer or drive (long-term memory). If you don't want them, close the window or delete them (short-term memory).

The way we process and retain information can significantly impact our mental health. When we receive positive feedback or do something good, we tend to forget it quickly. However, when we hear negative comments or experience traumatic events, we tend to store them in our long-term memory and dwell on them repeatedly.

The journey towards healing and self-discovery is not easy and can be complicated. One of the crucial steps in this journey is to reprogram your mind by eliminating harmful thoughts. These damaging thoughts can stem from various sources, such as past traumas, rejections, broken beliefs, and negative experiences that hold you back and erode your self-confidence. You must identify and address these deep-rooted issues to heal and move forward. This may involve working with a therapist or counselor, practicing mindfulness and self-reflection, and developing healthy coping mechanisms. It may also include confronting painful emotions, memories, and beliefs, which can be uncomfortable and challenging.

A Renovated Mind

I have heard this passage of scripture being preached numerous times, and it has become so familiar to me that I have even memorized it and often quoted it. However, I never fully grasped what it means to be transformed by renewing my mind. It was not until one day, when God took me on a journey through His Word, that I began comprehending the true significance of each word in this passage.

As I continued to study and meditate on the scripture, I gradually began to see the revelation and understand how to be transformed. The more I explored and delved into each word, the more I realized the depth of its meaning. It was like a veil was lifted from my eyes, and I could see things in a new light I had not seen before.

So, I humbly ask you to bear with me as we embark on this journey together and explore each word in this passage in greater detail. I believe that as we delve deeper into the meaning of these words, we will gain a greater understanding and insight into what it truly means to be "transformed by renewing our minds."

Transform

The Greek word "Metamorphosis" means "a total complete change from the inside out." This word perfectly describes the transformation a butterfly goes through. It starts as a creepy crawling caterpillar, enters the cocoon, the defining stage of its life, and emerges as a beautiful butterfly, gracefully soaring through the air.

But what's even more fascinating is that we, as human beings, also have the power to transform ourselves. Not into butterflies, of course, but into the holy person God has ordained us to be. However, this transformation does not happen overnight or all at once. It's a long and continuous process that takes a lifetime of effort and dedication.

As my mother used to say, "Just keep on living." The more we live, the more we will evolve and transform. This process is possible, and God wants us to change completely. We must remember that the change we seek will not come quickly, but it's worth pursuing and likely as long as we keep moving forward.

Renewed

The Greek word "Ananeomeno" encompasses the ideas of renovate, refresh, recondition, and restore. Of all these definitions, the one that strikes me as the most powerful is "renovation." Watching HGTV, I am constantly inspired by the stories of homeowners who transform their old, outdated spaces into stunning, modern homes. These homeowners recognize that their living situation is no longer functional and needs a complete overhaul. They call in a team of experts to help them with the renovation process, which can often be challenging and complicated. However, these homeowners persevere, and when the renovations are finally complete, they are overjoyed with the results. The once outdated and dysfunctional parts of their homes have been reborn, and they now have a fresh, new space that meets all their needs.

The Mind

The Greek word "Nous" or "Noos," is the center of a person's attitudes, thoughts, feelings, and actions. When most people hear "mind," they typically think of the brain and thought patterns. However, the true definition is much broader. Our mind refers to all parts of us and is the very essence of who we are as individuals. Our thoughts, actions, feelings, purpose, and desires are all interconnected within our minds.

So now, when we read the scripture, "Do not be conformed to the patterns of this world anymore but be completely changed by the renovating of your thoughts, emotions, purpose, and desires," we can see that it speaks to the power of our mind. Sometimes, we may face difficult situations or circumstances that try to keep us stuck in a negative cycle of thoughts, emotions, actions, and desires. These patterns can make us believe we are not good enough or that nobody loves us. However, these are lies from Satan and not from God.

It is essential to confront and change these lies into God's truth about us. We can do this by renewing our minds through positive affirmations, reading scripture, and meditation. By doing so, we can transform our thoughts, emotions, and desires to align with God's will for our lives.

There were times when I would experience negative thoughts that made me believe that I was not deserving of love. These thoughts had such a strong hold on me that I often acted in a way that prevented me from getting close to anyone. I would self-sabotage any potential relationship that came my way because I believed that I was not worthy of love and that no one would ever truly accept me for who I was.

It took me years of struggling with these negative thoughts and behaviors before I stumbled upon a passage in the Bible that completely changed my perspective. The passage was from the book of Jeremiah, chapter 1, verse 5 NIV, where God says, "Before I formed you in the womb I knew you, before you were born I set you apart; I appointed you as a prophet to the nations."

Reading these words was a revelation for me. I realized that I had been allowing my negative thoughts and beliefs to control my life for far too long. But here was God, telling me that I was chosen, unique, and loved. That realization was a turning point for me. It gave me the courage to believe in my worth and let go of the self-sabotaging behaviors holding me back.

Today, I am in a much better place emotionally and mentally. Although I still have days when negative thoughts creep in, I remind myself of God's words and the truth that I am loved and valued. It has made all the difference in my life. Also, praying and surrounding yourself with people who will speak positively in your life, holding you accountable for staying focused, and watching your words can help. Renewing our minds can take a long time, but it is worth it, and no one should rush you.

However, the rewards of this process can be immense. By letting go of harmful thought patterns and beliefs, you can build a stronger sense of self, develop healthier relationships, and live a more fulfilling life. Remember, healing is a journey, not a destination, and it takes time, patience, and compassion. But with persistence and effort, you can overcome the obstacles in your path and create a brighter future for yourself.

I understand that the following chapter's topic can be challenging and sensitive.

Therefore, I want to take my time and approach it with compassion and sympathy, ensuring that I provide all the necessary information clearly and with grace.

CHAPTER 6
It's Behind Me Now

> *Brethren, I do not count myself to have apprehended, but one thing I do, forgetting those things which are behind and reaching forward to those things which are ahead.*
>
> — Philippians 3:13 (NKJV)

Forgiveness and letting go are two of the most challenging things many struggle with. It's not just saying "I forgive you" or "I'm letting go." It's a process that takes time, effort, and sometimes even therapy. We often believe that forgiveness is a sign of weakness, that by forgiving someone, we are letting them off the hook and showing that we are powerless. However, the reality is quite the opposite. Forgiveness is not a sign of weakness but one of strength. It takes great strength to excuse someone who has caused us pain, especially if that pain was deliberate or severe.

Forgiveness is not about ignoring what happened or pretending it did not hurt us. It is about acknowledging the pain, accepting what has happened, and choosing to move forward. Forgiveness is a choice, and it is a choice that only we can make. It is not about giving someone else power over us but about returning our power. We free ourselves from anger, bitterness, and resentment when we forgive. We can let go of the pain holding us back and move forward with our lives.

When someone has wronged you or caused you pain, it can be easy to hold onto that anger and resentment, especially when the memory of that pain is still fresh. You may even ponder seeking revenge and making them suffer as you did. For instance, if your parents abandoned you when you were young, and now they want to reconnect with you, you may say you've forgiven them, but the hurt and rejection still linger. Or if your spouse cheated on you, you may claim to have forgiven them, but deep down, you are still holding onto that anger and may even have an affair yourself to get back at them.

Another example is feeling called to serve in ministry but discouraged by others' criticisms and opposition. You may begin to doubt your worthiness and question your assignment, leading you to abandon your calling altogether.

When we hold onto unforgiveness, it can significantly impact our lives. Unforgiveness can manifest in various ways, such as becoming cold-hearted, bitter, and irritated towards ourselves and others. This emotional burden can lead to physical symptoms such as headaches, insomnia, and digestive problems. Furthermore, it can affect our mental and spiritual well-being, causing us to feel anxious, depressed, and hopeless.

While we may feel justified in our anger, we must recognize its weight and consciously decide what we want to hold onto: rage or freedom. Jesus tells a powerful parable in Matthew 18:23-35, where a man refuses to forgive someone despite being pardoned. In this story, Jesus describes the consequences of unforgiveness as torture, which can burden us and prevent us from moving ahead in life.

Understanding that holding onto anger and hurt only hurts us is crucial. Refusing to forgive someone who wronged us keeps us trapped in our past, unable to move forward. Unforgiveness keeps the pain fresh. It prevents the wound from healing and causes us to repeatedly relive the hurt and anguish. This negativity affects our lives, robbing us of the joy of living the life God created us to live. However, forgiveness sets us free from our past, allowing us to be free once we forgive. Though it takes effort, healing and releasing these negative emotions is worth it.

Previously, I mentioned that I suffered hurt from my family members, which led me to question my existence. My mother's passing, coupled with my father's broken promises and absence when I needed him the most, made me feel alone and rejected. For a long time, I carried the weight of hurtful memories from my family. It made me feel broken, and I wanted to run away from them and never look back. However, during my defining stage, I read Matthew 6:14-15, where Jesus explains that our Heavenly Father will forgive us if we forgive others. This passage inspired me to let go of my anger and ill feelings towards my family and choose to move past them.

I prayed to God, asking Him to help me forgive my family for the pain and rejection they caused me. I also asked for help to forgive myself if my actions caused them pain. I didn't want to become sour because of the pain that surrounded me. Instead, I tried to grow through it in front of their faces so they may see His glory through me and be inspired to change.

After years of prayer and patience, God began working on me. Eventually, my family apologized to me for their actions and God even saved one of my sisters. Before my father passed away in 2018, our relationship grew better than it was before. I could heal and move forward since I had already shared my feelings with him. It taught me the power of forgiveness, even when it's hard. Sometimes, you must forgive privately before receiving and accepting public apologies.

I knew that I couldn't just leave my family behind. But more importantly, I knew that if I didn't forgive them, I would never be able to move forward and become the person God intended me to be. Forgiveness allowed me to release negativity and find hope and freedom. And it can do the same for you. If you're carrying the weight of hurtful memories, don't let it hold you back. Choose to forgive and find the freedom to move forward. You might be saying, "Nikki, you don't understand my feelings or know the magnitude of what I have been through," and you are right. I don't know, but I understand that you may feel like the situation is out of control, and it's easy to get caught up in the momentum. But holding onto unforgiveness won't make things any better. You have a choice: you can allow bitterness to take hold, or you can choose to embrace the pain and give it to God. With His help, you can turn your pain into purpose and find a way forward.

There is power in letting go.

My friend Emily had a traumatic past. She had experienced a lot of pain and betrayal from people she trusted, and it left her feeling broken and lost. She tried to move on, but the memories of her past kept haunting her, making it hard for her to trust anyone and form meaningful connections. Emily went through life with a heavy heart, constantly feeling like she was carrying a burden that she couldn't let go of. She tried to numb the pain by indulging in unhealthy habits, but it only made things worse.

Emily knew she had to confront her past and release the pain that was holding her back, but she didn't know where to start. One day, she met a therapist from her church group who helped her understand that she needed to forgive herself and others to move forward. Initially, Emily was skeptical, but she decided to try it. She began by writing a letter to herself expressing the pain she had gone through and accepting herself for who she was. She also wrote letters to those who had hurt her, expressing and forgiving her feelings. It wasn't easy, and Emily had to confront some painful memories, but she slowly started to feel lighter. She then realized that she had been carrying the pain for so long that it had become a part of her identity. However, with the help of God, therapy, her church support sisters, and self-reflection, Emily finally let go of the past and started anew.

Emily's life changed after that. She could form meaningful connections with people and no longer felt like she was carrying a burden. Emily found joy in the little things, and she was grateful for every day she had. Her journey was not easy, but it was worth it. Emily learned that letting go of the past is not a sign of weakness but strength. It takes courage to confront the pain, forgive oneself and others, and move on. Emily's life was a testament to that, and she was grateful for the opportunity to start anew.

Countless individuals, like Emily, are presented with numerous opportunities and assignments that God has set up for them. These opportunities await them to take the leap of faith, walk through the door, and seize the moment. However, sometimes, due to past experiences, we may not perceive ourselves as worthy or competent enough to take on these challenges. As a result, we pass on every favorable opportunity, make excuses, and continually look back at the rearview mirror of our lives. It's crucial to understand that our past doesn't define us. Instead, it has molded us into the people we are today. Our past experiences have shaped our character, values, and beliefs, and we shouldn't let them limit our potential. We must let go of the negative thoughts and feelings holding us back and look forward to a brighter future.

Every opportunity that comes our way is a chance to grow, learn, and achieve our goals. We need to embrace these opportunities and take a chance on ourselves. It's time to step out of our comfort zone and embrace the unknown. We should trust that we are worthy and capable of accomplishing great things. We need to look forward to what lies ahead and seize every opportunity that comes our way.

It's worth noting that there will be more challenging days than others, but we must remain focused on our purpose and destiny. Apostle Paul understood this concept very well. He knew he didn't have it all together and wasn't where he wanted to be, but he forgot those things in the past and focused on reaching for those that were before him. He knew his purpose and destiny were before him, not behind him. This is why he said, "I press toward the mark for the prize of the high calling of God in Christ Jesus" (Philippians 3:14 KJV).

No matter what we go through, we must be willing to adopt the same mindset that Paul and Emily had. We must let go of the past to embrace our true selves fully. We must keep pressing forward and never abandon our dreams and aspirations. Remember, you are stronger than you think, and your potential is limitless.

CHAPTER 7

Rejected, But He Accepted Me

> *For ye have not received the spirit of bondage again to fear; but ye have received the spirit of adoption, whereby we cry, Abba, Father.*
>
> — Romans 8:15 (KJV)

As humans, we all share a fundamental need for belonging and a desire to be accepted and valued by others. This need is even more pronounced in the age of social media, where the number of followers we have, the likes we receive, and our ability to fit in with the popular crowd can determine our sense of self-worth. When we don't measure up to these standards, we may experience feelings of rejection, inadequacy, and self-doubt that can lead us to change who we are to be more accepted by others.

It's worth asking ourselves why we place such a high value on the validation of others. When did the desire to fit in and be accepted become so important? Is it a result of our growth as social creatures, or is it a byproduct of modern society's obsession with fame, status, and popularity?

During my moments of quiet contemplation, I realized something. As children, we are taught to seek approval from our parents for everything we do or say. For example, throughout elementary school, I always strived to achieve straight A's; my mother's pride in my accomplishments meant the world to me. I was overjoyed whenever she praised me.

However, when I entered middle school, things changed. I excelled academically and maintained my A and B honor roll status for the first two years of middle school. Unfortunately, things worsened during the third year of middle school. I received an F in my science class during the second semester of eighth grade. I had always despised science, and I had never been able to comprehend the subject matter.

I remember being terrified when I saw the F on my report card. My mother had warned me about bringing home bad grades, and I knew I had let her down. Knowing I had disappointed her was crushing, because her approval of me meant everything.

I realized that I needed to make a change. I worked tirelessly to improve my grades, even going as far as to stay after school for one-on-one sessions with my science teacher. The hard work paid off when I was awarded the most improved student in science at my middle school's award ceremony.

The joy on my mother's face was priceless, and it made me feel as though all my hard work had been worth it. I received a B in the class, allowing me to maintain my A and B honor roll status.

Looking back on this experience, I now understand that my mother's approval meant more to me than just academic success. Now I see how our demand for acceptance and love from our parents is so robust that it becomes a learned behavior to seek approval from our parents and others to the point that when we are rejected, we will do whatever it takes to get it back.

Feeling accepted is a powerful emotion that can give us a sense of devotion, contentment, inner peace, and safety. It's a feeling of being valued and appreciated for who we are and what we bring to the table. When we feel accepted, we feel a sense of belonging and connection to others, which can be incredibly fulfilling.

On the other hand, rejection can be a difficult and painful experience. It can undermine our sense of self-worth and cause us to lose self-confidence. When we experience rejection, we may feel like we are not good enough or don't belong. This can be especially true if we are rejected by people or groups we care about, such as family members, friends, or colleagues.

However, it is essential to remember that rejection does not define us. We must not let it rob us of our confidence or sense of self-worth. Instead, we can use rejection as an opportunity to learn and grow. We can examine why we were rejected and what we can do differently. We can also seek support from others who accept us for who we are and will encourage us to keep moving forward.

Ultimately, holding onto our confidence and understanding its value is crucial. Our confidence allows us to take risks, pursue our dreams, and overcome obstacles. Hebrews 10:35

reminds us that our confidence has excellent rewards, and we must not let anyone or anything take it away.

Disapproval is Normal

Growing up, I struggled to accept that not everyone would like me, even if I held a prominent position or came from a wealthy or poor background. It was hard to understand why some people would not like me, making me feel like I was not good enough. However, as I grew older, I realized that I could not control what others thought of me.

When my mother passed away, I felt lost and struggled with my self-worth. I began to crave validation and acceptance from others, which led me to try to change people's minds about me. I became a people pleaser, doing things I would not normally do and changing who I was to fit in. However, I soon realized that my need for acceptance was holding me back from fulfilling my true potential.

I had to learn to accept disapproval and use it to become who I was meant to be. Even though it was difficult, I knew I had a greater purpose in life, and I could not let the fear of disapproval hold me back. I had to learn to accept that not everyone would like me, and that was okay.

Jesus faced rejection and persecution but continued to fulfill his purpose here on earth. He knew the world would hate him but still followed his calling. In John 15:18 NKJV, He said, "If the world hates you, you know that it had hated Me before it hated you." This powerful message shows that normalizing disapproval can free us from the pressure of being liked and allow us to live out our true purpose.

We all have a purpose in life, and we should not let the fear of disapproval hold us back from achieving our dreams. By accepting disapproval, we can use it to become our best selves. Remember, we cannot control what others think of us, but we can control how we react to it.

No Longer an Orphan

When a child is removed from their home and placed into foster care, it can be due to reasons such as abuse, neglect, or other issues. Such children often face identity issues, feelings of abandonment, and rejection when placed for adoption. They may find it challenging to fit in with their new adoptive families and may act out or rebel against their new life. This is often because they fear that the love they receive may be taken away someday. As a result, they may push others away and engage in behaviors that allow them to keep their guard up and protect their hearts from the pain of rejection.

Believe it or not, many of you reading this book may have experienced similar things. Although you may not have been taken away from your family and placed in foster care, you might have been abandoned, rejected, or abused by someone close to you. This could be someone from your family, church, or an unhealthy relationship that left you helpless and alone. You might have wandered into unfamiliar places or made poor decisions trying to fill the void and find a place to call home. Trust me, you are not alone in this. I understand how it feels to be in this dark place. Because of the immense pain and hurt you might have experienced, it can be hard to see the new opportunities and people God is placing in your life. You may feel that your past mistakes or experiences define who you are and may hold you back from success. It can be scary to open your heart to new people or experiences because you fear they may leave you broken and alone, just like an orphan child. But I want you to know that being vulnerable and trusting others is okay. You deserve happiness and love; it is possible to find it if you let go of the past and embrace the present.

Romans 8:15 reminds us that after accepting Christ as our Lord and Savior, we are no longer orphans bound to fear and inadequacy. Instead, we have received the Spirit of adoption, meaning God entirely accepts and embraces us. Therefore, you are no longer an orphan. You have a loving Father who watches over you, cares for your every need, and accepts you like you are despite your flaws and pain.

If you are unfamiliar with Christ and would like to know Him, you do not have to wait until Sunday to give your life over to Him and become His child. Romans 10:9-10 (NKJV) says that you will be saved if you confess with your mouth and believe in your heart that God has raised Him from the dead. So, if you want to be saved, you can do it right now by confessing with your mouth and believing in your heart. One believes in righteousness with the heart and with the mouth, confession is made unto salvation.

Join me in this prayer:

> *Dear Jesus,*
>
> *I am a sinner, and I have sinned for far too long. I have kept You away from my life, and I have no power to save myself. But today, I chose to open the door and welcome You in. I gratefully receive your gift*

of salvation and am ready to trust You as my Lord and Savior. Thank You, Lord Jesus, for coming to Earth and saving me from my sins.

If you have sincerely prayed this prayer from the depths of your heart, I want to welcome you into God's family warmly. You are no longer an orphan but have become a beloved child of God, and this is a significant and life-changing event.

As a member of God's family, you now have access to all the blessings and benefits that come with it. You have a Heavenly Father who loves you unconditionally, forgives your sins, and guides your steps. You have a Savior who died for you and rose again, giving you eternal life and hope that cannot be taken away. You have the Holy Spirit living inside you, empowering you to live a life that honors God and helping you understand the truth of God's Word.

In this new family, you are no longer alone. You are part of a community of believers who will support, pray for, and help you grow in your faith. You have access to resources like the Bible, worship, and teaching that will help you strengthen your relationship with God and your trust in Him.

However, it is essential to understand that following Jesus will not always be easy. Many people may not understand your decision and may even oppose you. But do not be discouraged. You are part of an incredible family, the family of God, and you are called to be a light in the world, sharing God's love and grace with those around you.

So, my sister and brother, I encourage you to embrace your identity as a child of God and live your life with purpose and passion. Do not worry about fitting in or pleasing others. God already accepts and loves you, and that's all that matters. Stand firm in your faith and walk confidently in your true calling, knowing that God is with you every step of the way.

Congratulations!

By sincerely praying that prayer, you have made one of the most significant decisions of your life. You are now a part of the family of God!

I want to encourage you to take a moment and write down your name and the date you gave your life to God in the space provided below. This will serve as a reminder that you are no longer alone. You have a loving family who has adopted and accepted you and is cheering you on to victory.

Whenever the adversary attempts to sow seeds of doubt about who you are, remember this date and the boundless love that envelops you. You are not alone. You are a cherished member of the family of God, forever embraced in His love.

- Name: _____

- Adoption Date: _____

Welcome to the family!

CHAPTER 8

Sufficiently Chosen

You did not choose me, but I chose you and appointed you so that you might go and bear fruit — fruit that will last — and whatever you ask in my name, the Father will give you.

— John 15:16 NIV

Do you recall those days of your childhood when you used to play dodgeball? I still vividly remember those moments, standing there with my heart pounding, waiting for the team captains to choose their players. Being the last pick was the ultimate insult, making you feel like nobody wanted you. This feeling of being undeserving or not good enough can linger for years. However, what if someone chose you and handpicked you for your unique talents and abilities? What if someone saw your worth, potential, and value?

Choosing can be a defining moment, a turning point that transforms your life. Whether it's an employer, a friend, or a romantic partner, being picked means that someone sees you for who you are. They see the actual version of you, your good and not-so-good days. They acknowledge your worth and believe in your potential.

As human beings, we all have a deep-seated desire to feel accepted and wanted. It's a natural inclination to seek a sense of belonging and to be valued in our relationships and communities. However, what happens when we achieve this acceptance and still feel unworthy? This is when things get complicated, and the arising emotions can be conflicting and confusing.

Despite being chosen, we may still struggle with inadequacy and self-doubt. We may feel like we do not deserve the call of God on our lives because of the mistakes we have made, the countless flaws we possess, or the negative experiences we have had in life. We may hold ourselves back from pursuing relationships or careers because we do not meet the world's expectations or fit into its mold. The weight of these thoughts can become overwhelming, leading to feelings of anxiety, depression, and a lack of self-worth.

Looking in the mirror, we see our beauty and flaws. We notice the lines on our faces, the bags under our eyes, and the grey hairs that start to appear in our thirties. However, as we stare longer, we begin to see our unforgettable mistakes and the voices that tell us we are not worthy or enough. These thoughts can be paralyzing, causing us to doubt ourselves and our abilities.

But we must learn to overcome these feelings of unworthiness and accept the love offered to us. We must embrace our imperfections and understand that we are all flawed individuals. Our worth is not determined by our achievements or the opinions of others but rather by our inherent value. We must learn to love ourselves, flaws and all, and accept the love offered to us. Only then can we truly experience the joy of belonging and being valued in our relationships and communities.

As I meditate on the powerful message conveyed in John 15:16 NIV, I am struck by its profundity. The scripture reminds us that Jesus handpicked imperfect individuals to be part of His team of disciples, such as Thomas, who was plagued by doubt; Peter, who was known for his hot-headedness and brawling; and others who were flawed and lacked faith. Despite their imperfections, Jesus saw their potential and chose them specifically to be part of His mission to change the world forever.

This scripture holds a profound truth: God does not seek out perfect people, but rather those who are open and willing to come as they are, with all their imperfections, thoughts, and actions, and be ready to be used by Him for extraordinary things in this world. When God gave me the book title, He also provided me with an acronym for the word "chosen," which aptly describes the nature of His elect:

- C – *Created:* God created each of us with a unique purpose and plan.
- H – *His:* We belong to God, and He loves us unconditionally, flaws and all.
- O – *Own:* We are uniquely our own but also part of God's more excellent plan.
- S – *Special:* God considers each of us special and unique and has a specific plan for our lives.
- E – *Elect:* We are chosen by God, not because of our perfection but His grace.

- N – *Nation:* As believers in Christ, we are part of a particular nation united by our faith and love for God.

With this in mind, let us embrace our imperfections and weaknesses, recognizing that God can use us miraculously, just as He did with the disciples. Remember that we are all chosen, not because we are perfect, but because God sees the potential for greatness within us. He sees our flaws as opportunities for His grace to shine through.

Today, you may feel undeserving and insufficient. You may feel like you're trying too hard or not at all or as much as needed. But today, you are fully seen and known, and chosen by God. Today, just like yesterday, God still has you in mind, and His mind has not changed about you. He still has chosen you and created you as His exceptional elect nation, and you are worthy of carrying out His plan and dreams for your life.

CHAPTER 9

His Beloved

Love is patient; love is kind. It does not envy, it does not boast, it is not proud. It does not dishonor others; it is not self-seeking; it is not easily angered, and it keeps no record of wrongs. Love does not delight in evil but rejoices with the truth. It always protects, always trusts, always hopes, always perseveres.

— 1 Corinthians 13:4-7 NIV

The yearning for love is a universal thread that weaves through the fabric of our existence. It's an innate desire, a primal need that resides in all of us. We all long to be loved and cherished by those who matter most: spouses, parents, church family, friends, and children. And we yearn to give love, hoping it will be reciprocated. But what exactly is this thing we call love?

Love is a complex and multifaceted emotion that can take various forms, each with unique characteristics. It can be a gentle and tender gesture that makes us feel cared for, a sign of respect and admiration that inspires us to be our best selves or a physical touch that conveys intimacy and connection.

However, love can also be a source of pain and heartache when we do not receive it as we expect or desire, causing us to resist love or feel unworthy of it.

Amidst love's challenges, it is crucial to acknowledge its transformative power. Love can heal our deepest wounds, inspire us to become better versions of ourselves, and fill our lives with joy and fulfillment. Yet, accepting love is not always straightforward, especially if we have been hurt. It demands vulnerability and trust to open us to love and allow it to work its magic. When we close ourselves off from love, we halt our growth and miss out on the beauty it can bring to our lives.

Alone, But Loved

In today's world, we are often pressured to believe that being single means not being loved or wanted. Society has created unrealistic expectations about relationships, making it seem like we are incomplete without someone by our side. As a result, many people engage in activities like casual sex, substance abuse, or working excessively to avoid feeling lonely. However, these distractions only serve as temporary solutions and fail to address the root of the problem.

Understanding that being single does not mean you are alone is essential. It is an opportunity to reflect on yourself and your relationship with God. God's love for us is boundless and immeasurable, extending beyond our past mistakes, brokenness, and feelings of unworthiness. Even when we feel weak and vulnerable, God's love is a beacon of hope that shines bright.

The Bible reminds us that God is close to the brokenhearted and saves those crushed in spirit. When we face life's challenges, we can turn to God's love for guidance and support. God sees us for who we are, with all our flaws and imperfections, and loves us unconditionally.

We do not have to earn or merit God's love; we need to accept it and allow it to transform our lives. When we trust in God's love, we open ourselves to a healing experience that can make us He makes us whole again. His love is a powerful force that can change our hearts, minds, and lives. We can experience joy, peace, and contentment that surpass all understanding as we embrace His love.

Jesus, the Son of God, came to show us the way and teach us about love. He spent time with sinners, outcasts, and those society rejected. He showed them compassion and love and called them to follow Him. Jesus came to heal the brokenhearted and give us hope for a better tomorrow.

When we feel heartbroken or unworthy of love, we must remember that we are not alone. We all deserve love and happiness; God sees and loves us just as we are. Trusting and allowing Him to heal our hearts can make us whole again. Seeking support from trusted individuals and professionals is also essential, as is trusting in His love.

When we allow God to work, we can experience a profound transformation that will change us forever. This process may not be easy and may take time, but with faith and perseverance, we can overcome our struggles and find peace and happiness.

The journey of self-discovery is not easy, but it is necessary. It requires us to embrace the place called "alone" and spend time in solitude. We can feel overwhelmed and anxious during these moments but must understand that we are still loved, valued, and cherished.

Allowing God's love to fill us during these moments can be a life-changing experience. It makes us realize the extent of our worth, regardless of the challenges we have faced. We can feel the warmth of His embrace and know He is always there for us, offering guidance and support whenever needed.

When we seek His guidance and help, we can receive the clarity we need to navigate life's challenges. We can find a sense of purpose and meaning we may have missed in these moments. Being alone does not mean being lonely. It can be a time for growth and reflection. It allows us to evaluate our lives, set goals, and determine what we need to do to achieve them.

Permission to Love Me

Do you put others before yourself? Do you ever consider that self-love is the first step towards loving others and knowing that we are loved? FLY: "First, Love Yourself." It is a profound reminder that self-love is necessary for well-being and building healthy relationships.

We spend every moment of every day with ourselves, yet some of us don't even like or love ourselves. In Matthew 22:37, Jesus said that the greatest commandment is to love the Lord your God with all your heart, soul, and mind. In verse 39, He stated that we should love our neighbors as ourselves. How can we fully love someone else if we don't even love ourselves?

We can become the best versions of ourselves by permitting ourselves to love ourselves and allowing God to love us. This journey of self-discovery and self-love leads to a stronger sense of purpose and a more fulfilling life.

Self-love is an essential aspect of our well-being that is often overlooked. It involves treating yourself with kindness, respect, and compassion and recognizing your worth as an individual. When you love yourself, you show up in the world as your best self and are better equipped to manage the challenges that come your way.

Self-care is one of the crucial aspects of self-love. It means taking care of your physical, spiritual, emotional, and mental health, setting boundaries, saying no when needed, and prioritizing your needs. Self-care can take many forms, depending on what works best for you. Be available for exercise, meditation, a long bath, or an enjoyable book.

Another critical aspect of self-love is self-acceptance. This means accepting yourself for who you are, flaws and all. It means acknowledging that you are not perfect but still worthy of love and respect. When you accept yourself, you free yourself from the need for external validation and begin to live life on your terms.

Self-love also means letting go of negative self-talk and self-criticism. It means recognizing that your voice telling you that you are not good enough is not the truth. Instead, you learn to treat yourself with the kindness and compassion you would show a good friend. You learn to focus on your strengths and achievements rather than your flaws and shortcomings.

Self-love can be a radical act in a world that often tells us we must be perfect. It means rejecting the idea that we are not enough and embracing the truth that we are worthy and deserving of love and respect. When we love ourselves, we can better love others and show up as the people God has designed us to be.

When we allow ourselves to accept the love and healing of God, we can move beyond the pain and mistakes of our past. In doing so, we can find our way back to our hearts by learning to love ourselves. At this point, our love becomes attractive to others, drawing the right people into our lives. However, this can also lead to the wrong people being attracted to us, but when we understand and know our worth, we are less distracted by these individuals or those who may try to bring us down.

It is not uncommon for that voice to remind us of our past mistakes or make us feel like we are unloved. But rather than listening to that voice, we can remind ourselves that we are the beloved of God and that He loves us unconditionally. His love for us is more significant than anything else in this world. We must look at ourselves in the mirror and say, "I love you too." An act of self-love can help us to remain positive, block out negativity, and remind An act of self-love can help us to remain positive, block out negativity, and remind us that we are worthy of love despite any mistakes we may have experienced.

When we tell ourselves that we love ourselves, we are affirming our worth and value as individuals. We are acknowledging that we are not defined by our pain, trauma, or grief, but rather we are worthy of love and affection regardless of what we have been through.

Remember, you are worthy of love and compassion simply because you exist. You don't need to earn love or prove your worthiness — you are enough just as you are. So, be kind to yourself, and remember that you are a beloved child of God.

We are worthy of love despite any mistakes we may have made or any pain, trauma, or grief we may have experienced.

CHAPTER 10

Embracing Your Style

> *For you formed my inward parts; you covered me in my mother's womb. I will praise you, for I am fearfully and wonderfully made.*
>
> — Psalm 139:13-14 NKJV

The word "style" is often associated with clothing, fashion, and beauty. However, style is more than just a superficial concept. It is a powerful tool for self-expression, a way to communicate your inner qualities and unique personality traits to the world.

Your style represents your creativity and distinct voice. It is a platform to highlight the talents that set you apart. Your style is unique, and it is what makes you special and valued. It is how you present yourself, your brand, and your statement to the world.

Embracing your style is a powerful act of self-empowerment. It is about boldly expressing your unique identity and being true to yourself. Remember, your style is not just about fashion; it is a statement of individuality that sets you apart.

In a world that often pressures us to conform, celebrating our differences and embracing our individuality is a powerful act of self-expression. Our uniqueness not only makes us attractive but also truly special to others. It is a magnet that draws people towards us and a testament to our inner strength. Remember, your individuality is what makes you truly special.

Our journey towards self-discovery and self-acceptance is not about striving for perfection. It is about embracing our authentic selves, celebrating our uniqueness, and recognizing our worth. Our individuality is a precious gift that we can share with the world, a testament to our strength and confidence.

It is challenging to let go of your fears, take risks, and embrace your individuality. The path to discovering your true potential and unlocking your full power can be unnerving but also gratifying. We often spend so much time trying to fit in, playing it safe, and avoiding controversy that we forget who we are. We sacrifice our uniqueness for compliance, and as a result, we never reach our full potential.

But if you want to truly shine and have influence in your life and the lives of others, you need to be willing to step out of your comfort zone, take risks, and let your true self shine. It might be scary and you might encounter resistance or criticism, but it is worth it. Because when you embrace your uniqueness and let your power value chain shine through, you will find that the world is a whole of possibilities. You will be able to achieve things you never thought possible, and you'll inspire others to do the same. Remember, your journey of self-expression and self-confidence can be a source of inspiration for others. Embracing your uniqueness benefits you and enriches the world around you.

Jane is a young lady I have been mentoring for some time now. She has always struggled to find her place in the world. While growing up, she tried to fit in with the popular crowd, even though she did not enjoy the same things they did. She felt lost and unfulfilled, always trying to be someone she was not.

As Jane got older, she realized that the problem was not with her but with how she was trying to present herself to the world. She understood that her true self was unique and special and that she needed to embrace her style to be happy and prosperous.

Initially, it was difficult for Jane to let go of her old habits. She was used to blending in and avoiding standing out. The idea of being herself and expressing her true feelings was terrifying. However, with time and practice, Jane began finding her voice and style.

She started dressing in clothes that made her feel comfortable and confident. She began speaking her mind and sharing her ideas without fear of judgment. Jane discovered that people were drawn to her authenticity and unique perspective. She realized she could make a real impact by embracing her style.

As Jane continued to grow and evolve, she was surrounded by a community of like-minded individuals who appreciated her for who she was. She no longer felt like she had to pretend to be someone she was not and could live her life on her terms.

Looking back on her journey, Jane realized that her willingness to embrace her personal style and uniqueness had led her to the happiness and success she had always wanted. She was grateful for the lessons she had learned and knew that she would continue to grow and evolve as she continued her journey.

In today's fast-paced society, people are expected to strive to achieve their full potential. Many individuals constantly look for ways to improve and grow, whether in their careers, personal lives, or relationships. It is crucial to take charge of your life and become the best version of yourself, stepping into your power and creating the life that God has already outlined for you before the foundation of the world.

It's important to realize that you may never fully discover who you were meant to be if you don't take the initiative to fulfill your potential. According to the renowned motivational speaker Dr. Les Brown, countless millionaires, bestselling authors, preachers, doctors, lawyers, business owners, and other successful individuals have never been seen or heard because they have already passed away. Many of these individuals had dreams and aspirations but never took the necessary steps to actualize them.

Pursuing your dreams and becoming the person you were meant to be is crucial to avoid this fate. This may require taking risks, facing challenges, and overcoming obstacles, but it's worth it. Remember, you can create your show and achieve your goals. So do not let fear or doubt hold you back — step into your power and create the life you desire.

Mastering the Value of Uniqueness

We all are different from each other, whether you are fat, short, skinny, or tall; some may even be physically challenged, which may have you running away from your distinctiveness, and it may even be hard to accept being different. Every one of us is a unique individual with our physical attributes and abilities. Some of us may be tall; some may be short, some may be skinny, while others may be overweight. Some may be physically challenged, making it difficult to perform everyday tasks. It is natural to feel overwhelmed by our differences and wish we were like everyone else. However, we must remember that we were not created to be the same. Imagine how dull the world would be if we all dressed alike and looked the same! It is our differences that make us attractive and help us to learn from one another.

Our unique attributes and abilities are essential for progressing and creating a better world. We must embrace and develop the qualities that make us who we are, as they are necessary to fulfill our purpose. Let us not be afraid of our individuality but rather celebrate it and use it to impact the world positively. But we were not created to be the same way. If we were, then we would all dress the same and look the same. Our differences are what allow us to evolve and help each other grow. We each have unique qualities that are necessary to improve the world, and we must accept theser qualities to fulfill our purpose as individuals chosen by God.

I want to share five key points to help you master your unique self.

1. Own who you are.

Coming to terms with one's identity can be an enormous challenge. However, accepting and owning who you are is pivotal to achieving a sense of belonging. Refusing to acknowledge your true self can lead to an overwhelming feeling of being set apart from others, which can be burdensome and discouraging.

2. Stop compromising who you are and set boundaries.

Establishing boundaries is crucial for personal, professional, and spiritual well-being. It means prioritizing your values and protecting your true self. A lack of boundaries can leave you vulnerable. Create a safe space by setting clear boundaries. It is not selfish but an act of self-care. Take time to determine your boundaries, confidently say " No," and communicate effectively. "Matthew 5:37 NKJV says, "Let your communication be, Yes, Yes; No, No, for whatsoever is more than this cometh of evil."

3. Find your Twelve.

"Find Your Twelve" is a concept that emphasizes the significance of finding a community that shares your interests and values. It is inspired by the story of Jesus, who handpicked twelve men to follow Him and spread His message. Similarly, it is essential to surround yourself with like-minded people who will support, guide, and understand you as you embark on a journey of self-discovery. "Find Your Twelve" is a call to action that urges you to connect with individuals who share your common purpose and interests to help you grow, learn, and achieve your goals.

4. Embrace your beliefs and do not change.

Holding on to your beliefs and values without compromising them to align with others' perspectives is essential. By embracing your beliefs, you stay true to yourself and your convictions. It is necessary to stand firm in what you believe in, even if it means going against the opinions of others. Staying true to your beliefs will lead to a more fulfilling and authentic life.

5. Accept criticism and rejection into your life.

It is essential to cultivate a mindset that is receptive to criticism and rejection. This means being willing to listen to feedback, even if it is negative, and using it as an opportunity to gain experience and grow. Additionally, accepting rejection gracefully can help you develop resilience and persistence in the face of setbacks. Remember that criticism and rejection are not a reflection of your worth as a person but rather a chance to improve and become better.

Throughout my life, I have struggled to find my place in society and the church. I often felt like I was trying to fit into someone else's mold, bending and adapting to meet their expectations. However, as I matured, I realized that my unique style and personality made me stand out. I started embracing my quirks and mannerisms, which allowed me to tap into my true self and let my authentic voice shine through.

This newfound confidence allowed me to break free from societal norms and expectations imposed on me by the church. I no longer needed to conform to a particular look or behavior to fit in. Instead, I started celebrating my individuality and expressing myself in a way that felt true to me and my faith. Whether through my fashion choices, hobbies, or how I interact with others, I am proud of the person I have become.

By embracing my unique style, I have felt more confident and comfortable in my skin. I no longer feel I must hide my true self or pretend to be someone I'm not. My style reflects who I am, allowing me to express myself in a way that feels authentic. Embracing my individuality has also given me a more profound sense of purpose and meaning. I now think I have a unique contribution to make to the world and that my individuality should be celebrated, not hidden.

If you are struggling with accepting your style, I encourage you to take the time to explore who you are and what makes you unique. Embrace your quirks and mannerisms, and don't be afraid to express yourself in a way that feels true to you. Remember that your individuality is something to be celebrated, not hidden. By embracing your true self, you will find the confidence and courage to live on your terms and positively impact the world.

CHAPTER 11

Be Unapologetically You

Find out who you are and do it on purpose.

— Dolly Parton

There is nothing more breathtaking than discovering your identity and embracing it fully. It is the essence of life itself. However, why do we constantly conceal our authentic selves from the world? Why do we allow the media to dictate our identity based on the number of followers, likes, and comments we receive when God has revealed our true purpose? It is time to break free from society's expectations and embrace the real you.

Being unapologetic means persistently pursuing yourself, having the courage to pull back all the cover-ups of who humanity has told and taught you to be, and being entirely upfront with the real you. In this period of traveling and becoming unapologetic, you will not be a different person.

No, your hands will not be new, nor will your feet, and you will not be in another body unless you decide to lose weight or get some cosmetic surgery. No, sis, no, bro. You will still be in the same body. Still, when you have an unapologetic mindset, you are choosing to accept no longer being a copy version of someone's ideal version of you, rather than standing in your raw feelings and no longer needing to live in secret, refraining from exposing yourself due to fear of rejection and ridicule.

Why not just live?

In this book, I boldly shared about my chameleon days when I tried to hide the best parts of me by changing them to what people wanted me to be because of the root of fear. I finally refused to let others dictate my identity and embraced my true self. I stopped talking down to myself and realized my worth. For years, I sought validation and acceptance from others, but I now know that self-acceptance and self-love are more important. I have learned that seeking validation from others is not love but a mistake that can lead to losing oneself.

Growing into that place mentally where you are entirely unashamed with who you are is a rewarding journey; it allows you to live more freely and contentedly when you have finally let go of the pressure of people's perceptions of you. It gives you peace like no other; you start to live a little differently, unyielding to this world's way of opinions but more yielding to God's truth about you, which is such a liberating feeling.

Face and Check It

Embracing your true self is a powerful and liberating feeling. But to do so, you must confront the things holding you back from realizing your potential as God's chosen one.

The **first** step towards this goal is to identify and face your obstacles and examine what has prevented you from being unapologetically yourself. It could be an old relationship you are still clinging to, fear of rejection, or crippling insecurities that are keeping you from moving forward. Whatever it may be, it is crucial to let it go.

Hebrews 12:1 NKJV boldly states, "Let us lay aside every weight and the sin which so easily ensnares us and let us run with endurance the race that is set before us." This scripture is critical, and you may have heard it at church many times. They talk about the sinful part of this scripture, which is essential, but before we get to the immoral part, we must first lay aside the weight. Sin is the result of the weight we carry. For example, when kept for too long in our hearts, anger causes us to act out in destructive ways such as fighting, killing, etc.

We must let go of whatever the weight is that will keep us from being and living the life that God has destined for us to live. It is time to take action, let go of the baggage, and embrace your true self with confidence and courage. Face and overcome everything holding you back from living life to the fullest and being content. Do not let the fear of rejection or ridicule dictate your identity. You are worthy of self-acceptance and self-love. Seek validation from within yourself, not from others. Remember, God wants you to live a life free from unnecessary burdens. Take the first step towards becoming unapologetic and let go of everything holding you back.

The **second** step is crucial: getting to know yourself. Discovering who you are at the core is one of the essential things in life. It is not always easy, but it is necessary to form meaningful connections with others and live a truly fulfilling life.

You must understand your likes and dislikes, what brings you happiness, what frustrates you, and what profoundly moves your heart. Reflecting alone and connecting with God can help you answer these questions and gain a deeper self-awareness. I have personally found that spending time with myself has transformed my life.

As a woman of faith, taking myself out on dates has been enlightening. Being alone has allowed me to connect with God and see life from His perspective. It is essential to take time for yourself, even if that means letting go of things that do not align with who you are. Embrace your uniqueness and let go of anything holding you back from getting to know your true self. Remember, your journey is yours alone, so make it beautiful.

The **third** step is to uncover the real you! Now that you have identified and addressed the issues holding you back, it is time to remove your disguise and embrace who you are. Your self-bashing disguise may have been used as a defense mechanism due to low self-esteem, or your laughing disguise may have been used to hide your pain behind jokes and laughter. The quiet disguise helped you bottle up your emotions, but it's time to say goodbye to all of them.

You were created to shine like a light, as Matthew 5:14-16 (NIV) mentioned, "You are the light of the world. A town built on a hill cannot be hidden. Neither do people light a lamp and put it under a bowl. Instead, they put it on its stand, giving everyone in the house light. In the same way, let your light shine before others so that they may see your good deeds and glorify your Father in heaven."

Do not hide who you are or let anyone else tell you who you should be. You are unique and special, and no one else can be you. When you leave your hiding place, you will inspire others to do the same. So, let your light shine, and let the world see the real you. We are waiting for you!

Live Out Loud

Once you have taken the time to discover your true self and learn to love who you are, the ultimate step is to live out loud. What does that mean? It means courageously showing up as your authentic self without pretense or apology. It means embracing your unique qualities and quirks and celebrating all that makes you who you are.

Living out loud requires honesty with yourself and others about your likes, dislikes, fears, and frustrations. It means being open and vulnerable, even when uncomfortable or scary. In doing so, you create space for real connections and meaningful relationships.

To live out loud, you must also be willing to acknowledge your strengths and weaknesses. This means accepting that you are not perfect and will make mistakes along the way. But rather than beating yourself up or striving for unattainable perfection, you learn to embrace your imperfections and use them as opportunities for growth. Living out loud also requires a keen sense of self-worth and self-love.

This means recognizing and honoring your own needs and desires, even when they conflict with the expectations of others. It means setting boundaries and standing up for yourself, even when it is unpopular. Principles and values must guide your decisions and actions to live genuinely. These principles will help you stay true to yourself and navigate life's challenges with grace and integrity. Living out loud is not always easy, but it is essential to living a fulfilling, purposeful, and authentic life. So go ahead, be yourself, and live out loud!

Taking this step forward may not be easy for you, especially if you have spent years hiding away as I did due to fear of rejection, low self-worth, and feelings of inadequacy. However, I want to encourage you to take this leap of faith. God has a unique purpose and calling for you, and you must fulfill it. You do not owe anyone else anything other than your commitment to God. He created you with a specific purpose, and you are responsible for fulfilling it. You may feel that what you have now or who you are is not enough, but that is not true. Who you are and what you have is more than enough for God to use. He can accomplish remarkable things through you, but you must be ready to live out loud and embrace your true self. Remember that you have been chosen for a specific reason unique to you. Do not let fear hold you back from fulfilling your destiny.

As I found the courage to confront my fear of rejection, I embarked on a journey of self-discovery that led me to realize the strength and potential that lay dormant within me. It was not an easy journey, but with God's divine guidance and unwavering support, I confidently embraced the calling of an evangelist. Even though I was hesitant and wanted to hide or run away from it, I knew that God had chosen me for this purpose.

As an evangelist, I share His Word, encouraging and serving others. Through my personal growth, I found my voice and the confidence to share my beliefs and inspire others from all walks of life. It has been an incredible journey, and with God's help, I have achieved things I thought impossible. As a girl who lost both of her parents, suffered from trauma after trauma, and never saw herself as worthy of it, I walked through doors I never thought possible.

Looking back, I realize my journey would not have been possible without my painful experiences. They challenged me to face myself, grow, and become stronger and more resilient. I encourage you to do the same, to have faith in your abilities, and to pursue your dreams with passion and perseverance. When you do, I believe you will discover an inner strength and resilience you never knew existed and achieve more than you could ever dream of. Why? Because you are chosen for it, and you are enough.

Acknowledgments

I am grateful to everyone who has contributed to the creation of this book. Your support, encouragement, and expertise are the pillars of this project.

I owe a debt of gratitude to my family, who have stood by me throughout the writing process. Their unwavering support and belief in me motivated me to deliver the best work possible.

My sincerest thanks to the Trilogy/TBN family, which has edited and published the manuscript. Your guidance and feedback were invaluable in refining and improving it. Without your expertise, this book would not have come to fruition.

To all the experts, professionals, and individuals who shared their knowledge and unique insights with me: I am grateful for your contributions. Your expertise added depth and credibility to this work, and I feel honored to have had the opportunity to learn from you.

Finally, a heartfelt thank you to the readers who will pick up this book and give it a chance. Your interest and support mean everything to me. I hope this work resonates with you and inspires you in your endeavors.

Milton Keynes UK
Ingram Content Group UK Ltd.
UKHW011457260824
447446UK00015B/1178

THE ELEPHANT IN THE ROOM

Simon Bardwell

Copyright © 2022 Simon Bardwell

All rights reserved

The characters and events portrayed in this book are fictitious. Any similarity to real persons, living or dead, is coincidental and not intended by the author.

No part of this book may be reproduced, or stored in a retrieval system, or transmitted in any form or by any means, electronic, mechanical, photocopying, recording, or otherwise, without express written permission of the publisher.

ISBN-13: 9798364775153

Cover design by: Violeta Nedkova

To Chris Brookes, thank you for the conversation that led to this book!

TOM

My name is Tom. This story may have happened. Who is to say now that it did not? We did some crazy things during that war, I can tell you. I am the last man from that team. I am heading towards the hidden life of our maker and spending my last days in a rather peculiar nursing home. I don't like to call it a hospice – that makes it sound too final. The nurse says it would be good for me to have a project as it keeps the mental processes active. She says she wants to be anonymous. Like the Nurse With No Name, I guess she could get into trouble for letting me express myself! Anyhow, all I have to do is press play and speak into this contraption. "Like this," she says. That was her. Clever, isn't it? Whatever happens, this will be my last project. I hope you like it. She says not to worry if I fluff the words, she will get her nephew to sort it out. He is a journalist, fancy that!

CHAPTER 1
SO SECRET EVEN UNCLE SAM DOESN'T KNOW

I first learnt about my new posting in 1942. I had been in the RAF at Biggin Hill, flying Spitfires on repeated missions. We didn't like to admit it, but it scared the living daylights out of us day after day. I used to smoke Woodbines and drink a lot of whiskey. It was the only way I could cope. Sometimes my hands would be so shaky that I trembled when I was lighting the tip of the cigarette. We weren't heroes; we were just ordinary blokes. It was easy to meet women because they loved the uniform and we seemed glamorous. We took advantage a bit, really. The sailors and infantry soldiers were not at home. We were, and that made us the lucky sods! We were the only young men in uniform down the pub of an evening.

    Nurse says I should keep focused and tell you about the elephant. It's a shame really as there are a few other tales I could tell. She says, "I know you, Tom. You will make it all a ramble and a scramble, and no one will follow it." The cheek. Still, she has a point, I suppose. Where was I?

Part of the problem with our nerves was because as soon as you took off, you were alone in the sky until you got home and had landed. The bomber crews were a team. If you were in a Spitfire, you were a one-man band. Of course, there was radio contact, but not much of that. I suppose if you are a modern reader, you might not know that a Spitfire was a small single-propeller fighter plane. I could still tell you the technical specifications, but all you need to know is that I was flying one of these small planes and the purpose was to defend or attack. But this story is not about that.

You see, I had a change of direction. It was after I had a mishap coming back to Biggin Hill after a mission. I thought everything had gone swimmingly: I had not suffered a direct hit and therefore had survived a scary dogfight. Well, that is what I thought as I descended towards the runway. I was impatient to get back on the ground. I was coming in a bit quick, but normally that would not matter. Except I did not know that my landing gear, the wheels, could not release. I was committed to landing and yet had no wheels to land on. I tried my best to pull her (the plane) up again and failed. So, I did a skidding belly flop along the runway, screeching and sparking as I went. Then I came to a shuddering stop.

I was still alive! That was good, but the plane was on fire. I blacked out then and did not see all that happened next. My mates told me that the ground crew were able to rescue me, but only with great difficulty. They said it was just as well that I had passed out. When I was dragged out of the cockpit, my legs were still on fire and I had to be doused.

I don't mind telling you the aftermath was not good. There was a lot of pain, and I was holed up in hospital for a long time. People came to visit me, and I kept talking as if I was going back to fly. They humoured me to begin with. Then eventually they kept falling silent. It would happen if I was talking about when I would be back on duty. After some time, I got the hint. The biggest hint was an envelope – a big brown envelope with OHMS on it. That stands for On His Majesty's Service. I don't suppose people know that these days. It was a very official-looking letter telling me that I wasn't going to be on active service anymore, and that I was to report to a new officer in command after a period of enforced leave. That's when they tell you that you've got to have time off, even though you don't want it. Nowadays they call it gardening leave. Nobody had the guts to tell me to my face. I suppose that's not so surprising, is it? In war, it is quite normal for people to concentrate on the active people who can make a difference. If you're injured, everyone is very kind but also distant. Well, gardening leave lasted for two months. At the end of it, I was getting very impatient and was dying to get back to something active. At the end of the two months,

I heard word that I had to report to somebody. Although it came in that official envelope I told you about, it was unusual because it told me to meet this person in a pub in Cambridge. It said that I was to be interviewed to assess my suitability for a special post. It didn't say what the post was, and it strangely said that I mustn't talk to anyone about the meeting or tell anyone where I was going. It went through my head that it may even have been a joke.

One hot day in May, I travelled from Walthamstow to Cambridge by train. Walthamstow is where my folks lived. I had been getting under their feet. My mum had been very encouraging, but my dad had been grumpy and just sat there with his pipe day after day, hardly saying anything to me. It was making me feel that I really needed to get away from them.

It took me a while to find the pub, which was on the outskirts of town and called the Creaking Gibbet. A charming name for a pub, don't you think? It was in a desperate part of Cambridge, I can tell you. I had expected to find a load of academics there, but it was filled with workmen. But there was one bloke in a suit who really stood out from the others. I had expected somebody in uniform. Instead, there was this man. I was filled with doubt, thinking that this was a perhaps a practical joke. But it would have had to have been very elaborate. I didn't think any of my mates would be capable of such precise planning.

Nurse is saying I should be more descriptive in my approach. I would like to know what she knows about writing at all, but never mind. She has had a look at what I've produced for her nephew, the journalist, so far. And she said to me I should make it so that the characters speak to each other as that's more interesting. I said to her, "That's funny because I was just about to do that."

I walked into the pub, and everyone was happily drinking. It wasn't one of those situations where everyone turns and looks at you. Nobody looked round. As I said, I deduced that my man was the one in a suit. I scanned the room, and he really stood out. I thought I would take a punt, so I walked up to him and said, "You must be Alfred Bonas?"

He gave me a scrutinising look and paused before he said anything. "Yes, I am he. Who are you?"

"I have come about the letter," I said. I thought I was being clever.

Let's try it how the nurse's nephew suggests.

#

"I came to see you about the letter," Tom said.

"Have you now?" The man looked at Tom as if he wanted to be sure before he said much more. "And what letter would that be?"

"I suspect you know full well. My name is Tom Hope. I'm here because I had a letter from my RAF command telling me to come here and meet somebody."

The man took out a packet of cigarettes. It was a new packet, and he seemed to spend a long time opening it. Maybe he was playing for time. He edged a couple of cigarettes halfway out and offered the packet to Tom. "Do you want one?"

"Yes, please. I don't mind if I do." He took one. He decided the gesture meant that he should sit down.

He still had not found out the man's real name. Surely no one could be called Bonas. Too near to Bone Ass for any sensible family. Tom smoked the cigarette. He had worn his uniform and was feeling out of place in the pub. The man had still not introduced himself.

Tom reached the point where he had to have another attempt. "This will be better if I am sure that you are the person I am to meet." He gave the man what he hoped was a pointed look.

The man just gazed at him. "Show me the letter."

Tom did what the man asked.

The man took the letter slowly. He read it and then threw it back on the table. He stood up and asked, "Would you like a pint?"

"May I have a pale ale?" Tom continued to peer at the man.

The ice seemed to be broken now. The man returned from the bar holding two pints. He pushed one towards Tom. He spoke, and this time was a bit more forthcoming. "My name is Phillip Phillips," he said. Then he muttered, "Until we are certain about you, all contact will be with me. You are not to speak to anyone else about this, not even your commanding officer. He can only know that you have established contact."

"It seems very cautious."

"That may be how it seems to you, but I can tell you it is completely necessary."

They sipped their beer silently, as if both had to wait to let the other one speak first. Perhaps ten minutes passed. It filled Tom with a desire to break the silence. He was just forming words when Phillips spoke.

"I should tell you why we have brought you here. We have been looking for somebody that we can rely on who can work discreetly and not be talking about it to all and sundry. It is highly classified work for the War Office. If we decide to take you on it is the kind of work that you can't even talk to your family about." Phillips paused and gazed at Tom. Tom found it unnerving, as if the man were playing some cat-and-mouse game with him. The silence continued.

Eventually Tom had had enough and asked, "What will it involve?"

Phillips looked around as if to gauge who might be listening. Tom felt that Phillips had tried to do it casually, but it just made him look furtive. Philip gulped down the rest of his beer and then stood up. "Come on, then. Let's go for a walk." He then went and stood by the bar and examined the menu that was pinned to the adjacent wall.

He waited for Tom to respond. Tom was feeling slightly annoyed because normally he liked to drink his beer slowly and savour it. Instead, he found himself gulping it down. It seemed almost a waste to do that, especially in wartime. Irritated about squandering a luxury, he stood up stiffly. He resolved to try to shake off his annoyance. Since the incident with the plane, he had found his lack of a role in the RAF very worrying. He needed a new job. As he walked toward Phillips, the man turned and walked away from him, onward and out of the bar. An observer would be forgiven for thinking that the two men were not connected with each other.

Once outside the public house, Major Phillips became very slightly more affable. He smiled. "Come on. Let's head to the park."

Tom did not know the area and so found himself walking beside his companion without a clue as to how far or where they were to go. Although this was the poor end of Cambridge, it seemed there was a park. It was small but had some woods next to it. Phillips said nothing until they reached the woods.

"If we take you, you will have to come up to Scotland. We have requisitioned an old house off of some laird. He wasn't that thrilled about it, actually. Still, there is a war on and there was nothing he could do about it. He turns up from time to time as if he wants to check on us, see that we are looking after his property. We have to bounce him out of there pretty promptly. What we are doing is so secret that Uncle Sam doesn't even know about it." He stopped, turned and looked at Tom, who had also stopped walking. The two men faced each other square on in the middle of the woods.

As they stood there in the leafy woods, they could hear the woodpeckers calling to each other, the unmistakable yaffle that Tom knew from his childhood walks. It appeared that Phillips – who was a major, Tom later discovered – had decided to trust him. He was to join the Special Operations Executive forthwith. He would be transferred immediately and would receive pay and rations from them. The RAF record would in fact show that he had retired sick, should anyone in that service make enquiries about him. He was not to have any further contact with his mates at the airfield. He was expected just to disappear and then turn up in Scotland. He was to say nothing. After he had left, they would arrange for a postcard to be sent to his parents from Dorchester in Dorset. Tom found himself nodding, wondering what he was getting himself involved in.

Of course Tom said yes. It seemed like there was no other option. If he stayed with the Royal Air Force, he would inevitably find himself stuck with a desk job and not being able to fly. This was at least offering something that sounded interesting, even if Major Phillips had been vague in the actual details. What he was being asked to do was a big step. He was to be uprooted from his family for perhaps the rest of the war, and who knew how long that would last? It would certainly be a new beginning if he took the job and left Walthamstow behind him. He also did not know how, or if, you could say no to something like this.

CHAPTER 2
SCOTLAND

Tom changed trains at Inverness. He was wearing civilian clothes, as Major Phillips had instructed him to do. The journey so far had been uneventful. He had an hour to wait at Inverness before he could pick up a small local train. For a while, he watched the pigeons fly around the station and then spent a bit of time looking at the WH Smith bookstall. There were a few Guild paperbacks on the wire rack, and he turned them over listlessly and tried to make up his mind if he could be bothered to read one. He spun the display backwards and forwards, trying to choose between *Portrait of the Artist as a Young Dog* and *The Postman Always Rings Twice*. A female voice behind him said, "Are you a young dog or a postman?" He spun around. He had not expected this.

Standing immediately behind him was a brunette dressed in the uniform of the Women's Royal Air Force, WRAF. She smiled at him.

"I am sorry, were you waiting?" he asked, feeling a bit flustered as before she had spoken he had not been aware of her presence.

She laughed. "Oh, only five minutes." She seemed to have a lightness in her manner. There was certainly no evidence of impatience.

"I am sorry."

"It really is okay. I have bags of time before my train gets in." She paused. He felt she was trying to decide if it was okay to speak to him and whether her intentions would be misunderstood. "Do you like reading?"

"I used to read a lot growing up. I am a bit out of practice, though."

She moved closer and he could smell the faint fragrance of a scent he knew well. "Can I help you make up your mind?" she asked, leaning over and plucking *The Postman Always Rings Twice* from the stand. "I read this one. It is quite gripping." Tom was having trouble concentrating. She was standing so near now. Plus, in his mind, he had placed the scent as the white soap his mother always used. He had never imagined that a younger woman could also use it, although of course there was 'a war on', and that would lead to economies being made. He absent-mindedly put his hand out for the proffered book.

"After you have purchased it, maybe you could buy me a cup of tea?" She smiled at him and stood and looked at him while she waited for his brain to catch up. Her presence seemed to have disengaged his normal thought processes. She picked up a copy of *The Lady* and *Woman's Weekly* and stood beside him as he fumbled in his pocket for his coins. She gave the man behind the counter a cheerful grin but said nothing. Tom felt she was secretly laughing at him – well, not so secretly! He handed over the money for the paperback and shoved the change and the book into his pocket. He waited for her to complete her transaction. He glanced sideways at her as she did so and took in more of her appearance. She was certainly a looker, as far as he ever thought about such things. The guys from the base would be envious. He found it unnerving that she had talked to him first, but maybe with being in uniform and everything she felt she could do so.

They walked towards the cafe together. It did not seem to matter either that Tom had not explicitly replied to her suggestion.

Tom looked at his watch. "I have about 45 minutes before my train leaves. That should be enough time for a cup of something and a cake. You are welcome to join me."

She nodded and smiled. "You can keep me company."

"Oh, I can, can I?" He looked at her and added, "You seem awfully presumptuous." He smiled so she would know that he meant little by it.

"I can be at times."

They arrived at the station tea room, a small cafe contained in one long hall-like room. There was a series of small round marble-topped tables with wooden chairs. They both homed in on the only free table. She put a bag on the floor and sat down whilst he put his suitcase down. He remained standing and looked at her in amusement. Then said, "It is counter service here. What can I get you?"

"Can we share a pot of tea for two? If they do toasted teacakes, can I have one, please?"

"Of course." He went and joined the queue.

It took a while to be served, and he returned to find her engrossed in her *Woman's Weekly*. She didn't put it down until he had finished offloading the tray onto the table. As he sat down, she put the magazine down and gave him her full attention.

"Thank you, you are very patient." She gazed at him. "What brings you to Scotland?" Neither of them had a Scottish accent, so it was easy to assume that he, like her, was not local.

"I am just up here to see some family."

"Are you in the forces?"

"No," he said, then decided that this was too evasive. "I am in a reserved occupation," he added.

She looked at him with interest but didn't ask any further questions at that moment. The phrase 'reserved occupation' could cover a multitude of sins, or it could be used in situations of a quite worthy nature. Tom felt that she was assessing him. There was a pause and then she started to talk about herself.

"We haven't even said our names yet. I am Jane. I'm on my way to a new posting." She laughed, "I couldn't possibly tell you where I am heading. I think I've deduced that we're on the same train, though."

He looked at his watch. "I am Tom." It felt peculiar to him to imply that he wasn't part of the RAF. Three months ago, he considered it his reason for existing. However, Major Phillip Phillips had taken care to impress upon him that there was no way that he should tell anyone where he was going. Certainly not some random stranger on a railway station. He laughed to himself because behind Jane was one of the Ministry of War posters, a cartoon by Fougasse with the slogan 'Careless Talk Costs Lives'. He felt like pointing it out and teasing Jane that she could be a German spy. Then he realised that even this was not possible. He picked up his teacake and started eating.

Jane was further on with hers.

"Were you hungry?" he asked, laughing.

"Yes, I skipped breakfast this morning as I did not leave enough time to get ready." She sipped her tea and gazed at him. "I hope you don't mind if we travel in the same compartment. I don't like being on my own in a carriage, and you seem a decent sort."

"Despite not being on active service?"

"That doesn't worry me. I expect you are contributing…" she tailed off and drained her tea. "I think we need to get a move on, you know."

Tom thought she was very bold, bossy

even. The trouble was that she was so damned attractive. He resolved to sip his tea and not gulp it down. He knew this was stubborn of him.

"I will see you on the platform." She picked up her bag and went off ahead of him. He saw her briefly talk to a man in a brown raincoat and then she disappeared through a door with a sign saying 'Lavatories' above it.

He still had five minutes before his train. He decided that if he took the briefing that Major Phillips had given him seriously, he should try to lose Jane here at Inverness before they got on the train.

#

When Tom got to the platform, he could see Jane waiting for him. He deliberately stood in the alcove between two parts of the station building. As he had his suitcase next to him, it was a cramped space and looked odd to the casual observer. He had selected this spot as he hoped he would not be seen from where Jane was. He watched her. She was on her own and there was no sign of the man in the brown coat. He told himself that he could perhaps be reading too much into what he had seen. She only had the shoulder bag that she had with her at the cafe. He thought it was odd that she was travelling with so little luggage. He felt maybe he was being ridiculous. That did not stop him from staying in his vantage point until the train came in. It could be heard well before it arrived. The steam train laboured its way towards them. It came into the platform underneath a small bridge, which forced the steam down and onto the platform for a moment or two. Jane vanished from view for a few brief seconds. Once the train stopped, a few passengers disembarked, and he waited for her to open the carriage door and board the train before he walked across and did so himself. He selected a compartment in another carriage. It was empty. It was not long before the train lurched into motion and continued on to its destination.

According to his written instructions, he was supposed to disembark at a small halt en route. He would be picked up from there. He fetched the piece of paper out of his pocket and realised with annoyance that he was supposed to have said something to the conductor at Inverness before they had departed. He sighed and wondered what he could do about it. If there was not another passenger for the halt he might have to hope that the train would slow down enough for him to jump off. He pulled down the window, leant out and looked down. He felt he might just get away with doing this if it came to it.

He glanced at his watch and calculated that he had about 45 minutes before the train would get to his destination. He got out *The Postman Always Rings Twice*. He sighed to himself – how had he let this woman dictate to him what he was to read? He let himself think about her for a few moments and then opened the book and started to read. It was a cracking read, but nevertheless after a short while he started to feel drowsy. He fell asleep, and the book fell to the carriage floor.

#

The train came to an abrupt halt. Tom woke up with a start. He leant forward and picked the book up. He stood up and quickly pulled down the window and peered out. He was at his stop! He threw the door open in the hope that the train driver would realise that he was going to alight. He then tossed his suitcase out of the carriage. It was followed closely by his cursing. He looked round the compartment to see whether he had forgotten anything and jumped down from the carriage onto the track. As he looked down the length of the train, he realised that he had been in the wrong part. There was a small platform about a carriage long that aligned itself with the first carriage of the train. On it, he could see a woman standing.

He picked up his gear and stumbled along the track then up a small slope and onto the platform. The woman was facing away from him, so he did not see her face. He could see that the road ran parallel with the track and that he could reach the road by a gate. So he ignored the woman and pushed the gate open with his foot. He was fairly sure he had got off at the right place. But, of course, because of the war, the place name was painted over. He looked at his watch. He was on schedule. He looked up and down the road, but there was no traffic and no car waiting. He noticed a bench, so he sank down onto it. He hoped that he had the right place. There wasn't much to be seen apart from a place for milk churns to be left. Presumably, the local farmers left their produce here for the train to pick up. For a few moments, he watched some birds on the telephone wire. All in all, he only waited about 10 minutes. It seemed longer, but that was the uncertainty. All of a sudden, a car came into view and came to a stop next to him. The windows were all down and there was one man inside. He had the look of an ex-military gentleman. He was dressed in civvies and had a lavish moustache. "Tom?"

"Yes, I am he."

"Fling your things in the boot then get in." The man paused and looked around with irritation. "Where's that bloody woman?"

Before Tom could answer, the car door opened and a woman got in. He was facing the front, so he turned to look. It was Jane! He said nothing and turned to face forward again. The car started.

The driver glanced in the rear-view mirror and addressed Jane. "Well?"

"He passed. He didn't tell me anything about where he was going. He is susceptible to women, though." She gave a little laugh at this point and wound the window up a little way.

Tom gave her an angry glance. He realised they must have been testing him to find out if he would reveal where he was going.

She put her hand on his shoulder and whispered loudly in his ear, "I hope there are no hard feelings. We do this to all the new ones." She gave a little laugh, took her hand away and leaned back in her seat. He couldn't see her now, and he wondered whether she was smiling to herself.

The driver sped up as if he was trying to make up for lost time. As if to explain, he said, "We have a briefing before supper."

Tom didn't feel very inclined to talk. His companions were silent as well. After about 20 minutes, they left the road and drove through an open gate. There were stone pillars on either side, with lions on the top. The gate had become detached from its fastenings and was lying on its side. There was a long driveway with a sharp turn at the end. The car came to a stop at what looked like a stately home. The driver turned the engine off and got out, leaving the keys in the ignition. He walked away and said nothing.

"I think he assumes I'm going to show you to your room. Grab your stuff and follow me." Jane took him right up to the top of the house. She pushed the door open on an empty room. "Here you go, this is your one. I will give you 10 minutes to freshen up and then I'll come and get you and take you to the briefing."

When she had gone, he had a quick look around and worked out that he had the luxury of a room and a bathroom to himself. He didn't feel like unpacking, so he just got his wash bag out and washed his face. He sat still for a few minutes, taking in his new surroundings. He felt that both his new colleagues had been extremely curt, laconic even. He hoped that they weren't always like that. He was used to a bit of banter and being part of a team. He waited for her to return.

CHAPTER 3

BRIEF

Of course, she came and got Tom exactly as she said. And so started the weirdest job he had ever had. All this time later and he was still not sure how much of it was still covered by the Official Secrets Act. How much can be told, dear reader, without getting into trouble?

The briefing took place in the kitchen. Just imagine the biggest kitchen that you have ever seen. One of those that you get in a stately home where the kitchen is manned by about 10 people. There was a lot of space. There were no kitchen staff around. They sat around a long wooden table. You could tell it wasn't going to be a long meeting because the food was already prepared and sitting on the side. Admittedly, the plates were on a warmer. The metal containers with the food were also on some sort of gas primer thing. The food was going to stay hot. He hoped that it would be a short meeting. He was feeling kind of dead beat from the journey.

They all sat around the table. At one level, the briefing was quite straightforward. Tom was introduced to the people he would be working with. It was a small, tight-knit team. There were six in total, which included Tom and Jane. The guy who picked Tom up from the station he had thought was a nobody, but it turned out to be Major Askwith, he of the moustache. It just shows that appearances can be deceptive. Tom felt bad to think that he had judged him to be a nobody. An errand boy (not so young) or a runner. He eventually learned that this was the kind of unit where everyone did a bit of everything. To Jane, it would not be at all surprising for him to come and pick her up from that tiny little excuse for a station. The Major had all his faculties and no obvious signs of decrepitude. As Tom had had such a long journey from London, he'd had a bit of time to think. He had started to imagine that all the people he would be working with would have had some sort of defect or other. Looking at both Jane and Major Askwith, he could see that he had been mistaken. Jane, of course, was quite a splendid specimen of womanhood. He could see nothing wrong with her. Well, in fact, he could see everything right with her. She had changed into civilian clothes and was looking quite a picture.

The other three team members were introduced. Tom noted that it seemed a requirement that nobody was known by their full name. Only the Major was known by his rank in addition to his surname.

Bob was a fresh-faced lad who looked as if

he was in his twenties. He had short blond hair and talked as if he had been to one of the posh universities like Cambridge or Oxford. He seemed to exude some sort of worldly knowledge. The Major said that he was one of the two scientists on the team. Tom wondered why there should be scientists, but he was not going to have to wait long before he found out.

The second scientist was called Clive, and he was a bit more of a pimpled individual. He was way beyond adolescence, in his 40s by the look of him. However, his skin was pocked with acne. The poor man had obviously suffered in this way for quite a long time.

With a flourish, Major Askwith then introduced the last member of the team. "This is Schmidt. He will help us with any translation or interpreting requirements. I'm sure Schmidt won't mind me saying that, until recently, he was a prisoner of war. He has, however, shown himself to be very committed to the war effort and has been passed to us on the understanding that he will be an asset. He is to be treated with every respect." Schmidt said nothing but blinked at them through a pair of wire-rimmed glasses. He looked entirely English and, according to Major Askwith, had been living in the country since the 1920s.

The Major said that for the benefit of Tom, he would give a summary of what the purpose of the team was.

Of course, he started by saying that

everything was top secret and nothing could be said about what was discussed once they left the room. He explained that they were part of the Special Operations Executive. They would be working on a small project called AWE, an acronym that stood for Alternative Warfare Enterprise.

Their unit had its origins in a Cabinet meeting at Downing Street. That is what he said, although Tom didn't quite believe that Churchill had been instrumental in coming up with the idea. For a while now, other units in the Special Operations Executive had been coming up with innovative ideas. The Major gave a few examples: an exploding rat that was sent into enemy buildings to cause carnage when it was set off while crawling through ducts; exploding pens; remote control ducks. They had even employed a magician to explain to them how they could create illusions to misdirect the enemy. Major Askwith seemed both scathing and amused by some of the stories, which he related at length. Tom was fascinated, but he also kept eyeing the food on the side and wondering what was in the containers. He was uncommonly hungry. The Major went on to say that their accommodation had been sequestered from a Scottish laird who had been very disgruntled at giving up his accommodation. It was gleefully explained that the laird was now living in a flat in Glasgow. "Oh, how the mighty have fallen."

Now the most interesting bit came. Major Askwith explained the purpose of their unit. He said that they were there to give misinformation to the enemy and also to develop advanced interrogation techniques. He said the work was on a 'need to know' basis and they weren't to talk to their colleagues about what they were working on unless they were specifically assigned to a team member. When they were off duty, say when they were relaxing in what he referred to as the mess, they were not to talk about any work at all. If they were working on a project, they were only allowed to talk to him or the other project members. He said, "If you don't know what you can talk about then you need to know but you can only talk about what you need to know to someone who already knows what you need to know. If they don't already know what you're going to talk about you don't need to tell them because they don't need to know it. Is that clear?" Tom tried to stifle his laughter. It seemed Schmidt also had a similar problem. Tom wondered whether he was also new to the unit.

"But who will tell us what we need to know?" Schmidt enquired.

"I will."

"Will you tell us everything that we need to know?"

"How would you know what we need to know? What happens if you don't tell us everything we need to know and you miss a bit out, and we know afterwards that we should have known what you had to tell us." Schmidt's accent sounded a bit strange. It kind of wandered back and forth between Oxford English and German. Tom looked at the man, trying to work out whether he was genuinely concerned that he might not know everything that he should know to do his job or whether he was taking the piss out of the Major simply because he could not resist doing it.

"Yes. Well, I will usually know what you need to know. But we are working on projects and sometimes we don't know what we should know before we start."

"Do you mean we will be making it up as we go along?" It appeared that Schmidt did not want to leave this matter unresolved. He had a determined look about him, as if he was going to press for an answer, come what may.

"I'm hungry," Jane blurted out. It was an entirely involuntary interjection from sheer impatience. "Some of us haven't had lunch because we had to go to Inverness." She looked around the room as if she was looking for somebody to join in the quest for food. She pointed at Tom. "I would guess he is hungry as well."

CHAPTER 4
SETTLED

Tom thought that it took at least three months to settle into any new posting. In Scotland, the first night was the hardest. When they had supper, everything seemed impenetrable. The building was poorly lit and confusing. His colleagues were very diffident and not easily drawn into conversation. Even Jane, who had been quite chatty at Inverness, was withdrawn. So, on that first night, he went to bed filled with trepidation. Of course, he had no choice. It was a war. This was probably the only job that was going to be available. But his instinct was telling him to leave the place. Duty, on the other hand, won out. He really could not afford to leave for all sorts of reasons. What would he tell his dad? His mum would just accept everything. His father, on the other hand, would be disgusted with him. He had lied to his parents about where he was going, and they thought he was going to have some sort of routine posting. They did not even know that he would be in Scotland. He had told them that he was going to Dorset. For him to reappear so soon would seem like a real admission of defeat to them.

Furthermore, would they consider it to be a desertion of his post if he left? All these thoughts were going through his head on the first night. He slept very uneasily. It did not help that the mattress was one of those horsehair ones that can get a bit lumpy from continued use. Halfway through the night, he had to get up and try to beat it into shape. He imagined that if he did that, it would at least get the lumps out. He had assumed that there was nobody sleeping next door. That was until he heard a loud voice through the wall: "Shut the fuck up!" It wasn't a voice that he recognised. He didn't discover until the next morning that it was the chef, Ivan. Ivan was nicknamed Ivan the Terrible. It appeared that this was mainly because of the quality of the food that was served up. Tom had been right, though, that the rest of the crew were spread out through the building. It was a multi-roomed mansion. It was unfortunate for Ivan that he was next door to Tom. And, equally, it was unfortunate for Tom that he was next door to Ivan. They developed a certain animosity towards each other. It never broke out into open hostility, just a series of little passive aggressive gestures that the English are so good at.

He made more progress with the other colleagues. Over time, it began to feel that Jane might even be a friend. To begin with, he had hoped for more than that. But any of the overtures that he made were batted back with bold indifference. She was quite a diplomat, though, and managed to do this whilst maintaining a friendly attitude. Indeed, she was certainly a woman who could flirt without intending to. Of course, Tom was unaware that she had five brothers and therefore did not necessarily view men as sexual conquests. Although Tom was slightly older than her, she seemed to view him as a brother rather than a friend. He really opened up to her over time. On a Sunday evening, they would quite often go to the pub in the village for a drink. It was quite a long walk there and back. He would find himself telling her many private things. She, on the other hand, was quite circumspect with him.

For example, she told him nothing of her personal life. He did, however, learn all about her choice of nylons and if and where they could be found during the war shortages. Also how to fake wearing stockings using eyeliner. He had worked out her favourite soap on the first day, if you remember, because it smelt the same as the one that his mother used. He was to learn what was her favourite perfume. She also liked to use him as a second opinion when she went shopping for dresses. There was endless talk of favourite books, and she would sometimes ask him to go to the talking pictures with her.

He never asked himself why it was like this.

For the most part, he enjoyed it, but it would cause him occasional difficulties when she was unexpectedly intimate in what she talked about whilst expecting him to take no action on his feelings. This possibly came about because she was the only woman working amongst these men. She needed an ally, and he was an obvious choice. Oh, and plus, she liked him. Tom was quite a sympathetic character.

She also had the capacity to shock him. He had been brought up in quite a puritanical manner. Both his parents were quite good-hearted, but they had high standards. For him, one of the most shocking things that happened in the early days was when they were walking along a coastal path. Unlike the South Coast, which was barricaded against possible invasion, the Scottish coast was relatively uncontrolled. There wasn't a lot of barbed wire or barricades to stop you getting near the water. They were halfway through a walk between two towns and making the most of a day away from base. At Jane's suggestion, they stopped for lunch. They had a couple of boiled eggs and Marmite sandwiches to share. Tom had brought a bottle of water, which was passed between them as they sat at the side of the sea. They had been chatting about who knows what. Well, Tom hadn't been paying attention.

Jane suddenly said, "The water looks nice." At this, she started to strip off her clothes until she was stark naked. She hid her clothes behind a bush and said to Tom, "Are you going to come in then?" She didn't wait for an answer and ran towards the water. It wasn't long before she was waist deep. Tom was shocked and couldn't believe what he saw. This kind of behaviour would have got him into deep trouble with his parents. The water was up to her neck now and she started to swim around.

"Oh, heck," he said to himself. "Well, in for a penny, in for a pound." He stood up and stripped off, having reasoned that he might as well join her; besides, he did not want to appear to be a prude. He put his clothes next to Jane's and then waded into the water. The water was pretty freezing, even though it was a sunny day. He shuddered slightly as he waded towards her. He was relieved that he couldn't see below her neck now as she swam backwards and forwards. It wasn't that he didn't enjoy seeing her naked body, just that he didn't want any sort of uncomfortable feelings between them when they were together. They only stayed in the water for about half an hour because it was so cold. They swam backwards and laughed, talked and splashed each other a bit. This incident was how he discovered how impulsive Jane could be. The moaning started as soon as they were back on the shore. She didn't seem at all worried about what he could see of her but became infuriated with herself for not realising that she had nothing to dry herself with. She disappeared into the bush that she had left the clothes under. She gave a running commentary as she tried to improvise, drying herself with bits of vegetation.

"This will do. There are some large dock leaves here. You could use something like this when it's your turn," the bush said.

Tom was waiting impatiently on the other side, praying that nobody would walk past on the footpath.

"Hurry up, Jane."

"Oh **** there was some nettles amongst that. I have been rubbing them and dock leaves against myself. What a blooming idiot. Tell you what, I think I'm going to just sit in the bush for a bit. I think the sun will do a better job."

"Haven't you forgotten something? I'm standing here like a lemon."

She laughed. "Are you sure it's like a lemon?"

"You know exactly what I mean. I am worried somebody's going to see me."

"Well, come in here then. There isn't anything you haven't already seen. Just behave yourself." It seemed strange to Tom that she made a point of saying that now.

The two of them spent about 20 minutes crouched on the grass. Jane eventually got fed up and said that she was going to put her clothes on. "I don't mind if they're wet. It's just ridiculous. I don't know what makes me do these things sometimes." He spoke some consoling words as she dressed. He started off trying not to look at her, but she was talking so much that in the end he just chatted to her as she went about her business. In this case, the business of getting her clothes back on. She stuffed some of her underwear in her rucksack, muttering something about not wanting to go round in soggy clothes all day. She waited while Tom did the same. Walking back to base wasn't too bad as the weather was both sunny and windy.

That sort of incident was part of the reason why she and Tom got so close so quickly. In those early days, she was certainly the most forthcoming member of the team as far as he was concerned.

Ivan the Terrible didn't like him at all and tended to just grunt at him. Tom felt that Ivan could have easily poisoned him if he wanted to. He was, after all, the cook for everyone. Fortunately, he wasn't that vindictive, though.

Of the other team members, to begin with he was closest to Schmidt. Schmidt was prepared to talk, while the others tended to just stay silent. Plus, the two of them would play chess together in the evenings after supper.

Slowly, Schmidt opened up to him. He was the sort of man who naturally played his cards very close to his chest. Maybe this was because he had had quite a rough ride in the country so far. His family had been singled out for abuse because he was German in a time of war. Yes, he had been a resident in England since 1922 when he came to university. He had studied English literature at

Oxford University. He didn't fit in there, though. He explained it to Tom this way.

"I wasn't like the other students. I wasn't from a moneyed background. Oxford was a scholarship opportunity for me. It was an extraordinary time for me, really opening up my view of the world. It was very difficult for me to keep up with everyone. Some of them would study really hard, but at the same time also play really hard. And then, of course, there were a couple of toffs who would just take the **** out of the system something rotten. They would always be going away for the weekend to some fancy house in the country. A bit like this one, to be honest. Very occasionally I would get an invitation too. I would sometimes get the impression, though, that I was invited as a kind of performing foreigner. Some of them had a dreadful, cliched view of what I should be like. On the other hand, I got so much out of university that I can't complain. I mustn't complain, in fact. I have a love of languages and studying English literature was a dream for me. Chaucer, Shakespeare, Dickens. These were all essential reading, including a more esoteric selection.

"Afterwards I went on to do my master's, again at Oxford. This took me up to the start of the war, there was a little delay before they got organised. Then they interned most of the Germans already living in the country. I have to tell you: my family were totally innocent of any chicanery. Yet we were all imprisoned. My mother, my father, myself, my sister. And what had we done wrong? Nothing. My father did his best to appeal against all this. Fortunately for me and my sister, he had a lot of friends in high places. We were eventually removed from the internment camp and put under house arrest. That was a lot easier to cope with. Things improved even further when our new master needed somebody to help with interpretation. I must say, since I've been here, they haven't really put me to work yet. It must come soon, I hope. All that I've had so far are a few documents that anyone could translate, really."

"That must have been hard. All that uncertainty."

"I think that is checkmate, Tom."

"How on earth did you manage to do that? I can never play and talk!"

"Were you trying to distract me by asking all those questions?"

"Certainly not!"

Schmidt stood up and asked, "Do you want another beer?" He continued to talk even as he left the room and then returned shortly with the beer bottles. "You know, we should help you develop that skill. The talking and concentrating one."

Tom felt slightly infuriated to be told this. He felt that Schmidt was exceeding his reach as a friend. But Schmidt didn't seem at all concerned and so continued.

"I do think Jane and I could devise an experiment to help you with this. I'm going to speak to her about it."

Tom could only utter bleakly, "Oh, do you have to?"

#

In the run up to Christmas, Major Askwith had been very secretive. Everyone in the house knew that something was going on because of all the comings and goings. There were secret meetings with top brass, including, it seemed, government officials. He said nothing. He was increasingly distant over the few days leading up to Christmas Eve. By instinct, they knew that there was no point in asking any questions. Jane and Tom decided to go to the village on Christmas Eve. Tom was an agnostic, but Jane had some sort of vestigial interest in Christmas celebrations. At least this is what Tom deduced from her behaviour. Two days before Christmas, she had suggested to him that he go with her to midnight mass at the local Catholic church. In his experience, her suggestions were more like commands. He didn't mind. He enjoyed her company, and she was usually a laugh. Also, Major Askwith was so busy that the rest of the team had been at a loose end for some time. That meant, in effect, that Tom was willing to do anything she wanted. It would be a good break from the boredom.

The village church was two miles away and they had the choice of either walking or going by bicycle. Tom pointed out that the pub was quite near the church and that maybe they could have a drink before mass. Jane agreed but said that they mustn't be sozzled before they went in the church. Tom said he thought it was better if they walked. Jane agreed, as long as they could take a torch with them. This made sense as the road was quite narrow in places. It was very unusual to meet vehicles on it, but it would be worth being able to signal that you were there in the dark.

They set off early enough to allow time for them to have a drink. They walked in silence for a while until Jane opened the conversation.

"What do you think is going on?"

"I really don't know. I think Major Askwith was born secretive. I bet he wouldn't even tell his nanny if he did a number two in his potty."

"That's a disgusting image. Thank you!" She turned to glance at him as they continued to walk.

"You know exactly what I mean, don't you?"

She laughed. "Can you imagine being married to him? He is married, I heard him say once. When he writes home, he probably would redact the pages himself. Can you imagine it? He probably would say things like, 'Dear Binky, I want to rip off your blank blank. I have a massive blank blank, but you can't possibly imagine it because it is something I can't officially show to you. It is a pork blank that needs to be hidden. Prepare to repel boarders!'"

"You idiot!" He shot her a glance to see if she

was laughing.

"But what is really going on? That's what I want to know. I'll tell you what I guess, and you can tell me what you guess. I think we're going to get a prisoner. A real live one, not a practice run like the ones that we've had before. That's what all this secrecy is about, all this coming and going. I mean, it's been relentless over the last few days. I can't understand why they don't tell us, because we're going to be the ones doing the work. Well, what is your guess?" She turned to him expectantly.

"I reckon it's about Schmidt. My money is on the fact that they've found out he's a double agent. That's why they can't talk to us about it."

She stopped walking and looked at him. "Really?"

"No, of course not. Schmidt is our friend. He wouldn't do anything stupid. Well, nothing terminally stupid anyway. He specialises in the incomprehensively stupid."

Jane grabbed his arm. "Yes, we like him. We mustn't lose him. Maybe it's really for Ivan the Terrible. Perhaps they're going to see what he serves up at Christmas and see whether they should try him for crimes against humanity."

As they continued to walk, they were surprised to see two motorcycles and a vehicle approaching them at speed. They put the torch on and stood at the side of the road so that they could be sure they wouldn't be hit. The vehicles continue at speed. They didn't even slow down. There were two men in front of the car and one person in the back. They couldn't make out any of the faces or make sense of what uniforms were worn.

Tom said, "There's only one place they could be going. It must be important if it's happening on Christmas Eve." He meant that the road only led to the mansion they had just come from.

#

Tom didn't really know what he felt about Jane. He certainly liked her and loved spending time with her. His male brain had registered that she was very attractive, but at the same time he was aware that she was not interested in being his girlfriend. It was therefore perhaps a mistake to end up in a public house with her drinking on Christmas Eve. The pub was called The Angel. Fortunately for them, it would be only a short stagger, when the time came, down the road to the Catholic church. In the meantime, the atmosphere was good. The landlord had put up some simple decorations and there was a Christmas tree. Nothing too lavish, you understand, as befitted a wartime celebration. Just enough to make sure that you felt you were in the Christmas season. It was only their second time in the pub. They had novelty value as far as the regulars were concerned. Perhaps because it was Christmas and a time of goodwill to all, a few people offered them drinks. They were in the difficult position of being local but not being able to admit what their profession was. Tom noted that Jane did a much better job of fudging what her background was. On the spur of the moment, he said that he was a tree surgeon and that he was working on the laird's estate. This was not the most convincing of covers, seeing as he had the look of someone who could not get up a ladder easily. Still, the deed was done, and he had to commit to the part. He and Jane ended up sitting next to a rather drunk farmer and his wife. The farmer began to relentlessly question him about trees. For a few moments, Jane noticed the difficulty and tried to change the conversation to something more manageable. She was even slightly rude and shouted across the two men to the farmer's wife on the other side. The natural thing would have been to move to sit next to her, but Jane deliberately didn't.

"And you, have you got any children?"

"Yes, three of the little blighters."

Eventually, the men gave up trying to talk while the two women shouted across them. There was much talk of nappies and school. Tom was intrigued that Jane had so many questions for the woman. He realised what she was doing, of course. He was wondering whether it was a mistake for them to come here. Maybe they should have taken a car and gone a bit further, to somewhere where they wouldn't have been known. Jane's plan, on the other hand, was to get the farmer and his wife to have as many drinks as she could possibly manage. She reasoned to herself that if she did this then come next morning, they may remember nothing. She allowed herself to become a bit distracted by all this until suddenly she looked at her watch.

She stood up and grabbed Tom's shoulder and squeezed the material. She swayed slightly and said, "Come on, you. We have an appointment with the big fella." They bade beery farewells to the farmer and his wife and shouted Merry Christmas into the saloon bar as they left for the church. One or two others followed them.

Tom had hardly ever been in a church in his life. Therefore, he wasn't quite prepared for what he was going into. He had a couple of bottles of ale in the inside pocket of his heavy overcoat. He had surreptitiously bought these so that he could have a drink with Jane after church as they headed back. He was okay with the first bit of the service, which was all carols. The church was full of candles and most of the light came from them. The carols were familiar and he could join in with them. What came next seemed quite unnatural to him. There was a solemn procession, the altar boys preceding the priest.

And then the priest started talking in a foreign tongue. It took Tom a while to acclimatise and then he realised it was all going to be in Latin from then on.

He whispered into Jane's ear, "You could have warned me it was going to be in Latin."

"I just thought you would know," she said quietly. Then she added, "Just try and be patient with it all. For me!"

He found the booze helped. It kind of anaesthetised him from all the religion. When it came time for people to take communion, it surprised him to see that Jane went up. After this point had passed it all seemed to end very quickly. It was about one in the morning and everyone dispersed readily. It would take them about an hour to get home.

Jane seemed to have shrugged off the effect of any alcohol that she had taken during the evening. Tom was still feeling a bit fuzzy in the head. They set off at a brisk pace, impatient now to get to what they now called home. After a bit, Jane realised that Tom was making a clanking sound as he walked.

"What on earth is that noise?" she asked.

"Oh, I brought us a couple of bottles of ale for the walk home," he answered.

"I bet you haven't got a bottle opener."

"Yes, I have." He fished around in his pockets and brought out his penknife. They had come to a standstill.

He felt she was looking at him with amusement. But, of course, it was dark, and he couldn't see her face and he was wrong. Instead, she said, "Hurry up, I'm getting cold. I have a nasty feeling it's going to start snowing." He handed her the first bottle he opened. He had more difficulty with the next one and spilled half of it when he opened it. Jane silently swapped the bottles so that

Tom had the fuller one. "I think you need it more than I do," she said.

Fortunately, his instinct saved him from doing anything stupid. When he had still been in the pub, he had thought that on the walk home he would be able to kiss her. He knew from her tone that she was now impatient to get home and was not to be dallied with. And, of course, he was right. For the first quarter of a mile or so, they trudged along in silence. Slowly, she started to chat again. Whatever had been bothering her had passed. They tried to predict what the next few days would bring. Both admitted to feeling slightly strange about being away from home at Christmas. They knew that Ivan the Terrible would serve up some food tomorrow and hopefully it would be okay. His food was only terrible some of the time. There were some things he just couldn't master, but surely a yuletide feast should be within his capabilities?

They were still laughing about this when they reached the mansion. They had expected all the lights to be off and Tom had his torch ready. But the lights were still lit in Major Askwith's office. The car and the motorcycles that they had seen earlier were parked outside on the drive. They tried to let themselves in very quietly, although there was no need to be secretive at all as everyone knew where they had gone. There was just something about the fact that it was Christmas Eve and well after midnight that made them instinctively want to creep around. In the hallway, they could hear that Major Askwith was still loudly discussing something with what they presumed were the visitors. Jane wanted to stop outside the door and even eavesdrop, but Tom bundled her along. They both disappeared into their respective bedrooms.

Tom suddenly realised how tired he was, and he flopped onto the bed. He still had his boots on, so he stuck his feet over the edge of the bedding so that he didn't get it muddy. He lay there for a few minutes in a reverie. There was no doubt that he liked Jane. Now that he was home and not in the pub, he tried to tell his heart that it wasn't going to go anywhere. Was this one of those situations where he was better off accepting what it was and just taking what breadcrumbs of friendship she might offer him? He fell asleep for a while, but then his snoring woke him up and he pushed his boots off. He didn't bother to get into bed properly, he just lay on top of the bed and fell asleep in his clothes.

CHAPTER 5
FIND ME AN ELEPHANT

Major Askwith started the new year with a briefing. He never explained what the comings and goings had been about over the Christmas break. He did, however, have a new year project. It was January 1st. At the beginning of the briefing, they wondered whether maybe he had imbibed too much alcohol the night before. Most of what he said made perfect sense, apart from one subject: the elephant!

Let's start with the dull and boring part first. He certainly did. He ran through the current status of all the projects they were working on. And frankly, up until now there hadn't been enough to do. This had applied to them all. However, today he seemed to be full of newfound fervour, emphasising to everyone that what they needed to do was to get to the conclusion of these projects and not faff around anymore.

Maybe the dull and boring bit wasn't so dull, actually, as next he had an announcement about an incoming prisoner. Up until now they hadn't practised on anyone who was a live human being, apart from each other. Of course, interrogating each other comes with difficulties. Some people are better at role play than others, and some people are just useless at it.

The Major was delightfully vague about the source of this person. He was, however, 100 per cent German. They did not know how much English he knew, so Schmidt was going to be needed from the very beginning. Eventually, they would learn more from the prisoner than they learnt from Major Askwith that day. Afterwards, when they discussed it, they realised he had basically spent 20 minutes telling them they were getting a male German prisoner and that they would most probably need to speak to him in German. No questions were allowed. It was a marvellous fact that he managed to spread that part of the briefing out for a whole 20 minutes. There is a certain type of military person who can make anything sound very significant and of great import. To be fair to the Major, in this circumstance, he was not allowed to say anything of any detail. He was very excited, in fact. But he had enough sense not to show this to people. This particular project had come from the very top of government. He had imagined Churchill walking around the Cabinet Room, saying that he must have Major Askwith for the task. Nobody else would do!

And then we came to item three on the agenda. Major Askwith revealed that he would like Jane and Tom to find him an elephant. The ideal would be an elephant that was used to being around humans. He said that, because of this, he wanted to rule out getting one from a zoo right from the beginning. Schmidt was still a bit overexcited from learning that he was going to get a German to play with. He was the first to weigh in with the questions.

"Excuse me, Major, would you like an African or an Indian elephant?" he asked.

"Thank you, Schmidt. A very good idea. I think you should research that for me. Find out which one is best around humans. I'd like you to do that by tomorrow morning." He looked around the room and said, "I wish all the rest of you were as forthcoming with ideas as Schmidt."

Tom tried desperately to think of something intelligent to ask but was pipped to the post by Jane.

"Once we have found the elephant, we'll need to bring him back here?" she asked.

"Yes, of course he is going to be housed here. We will need to work out the precise mechanics of that. He will be in his own quarters some of the time." That last bit sounded mysterious to everyone. Why wouldn't the elephant be in his, or her, quarters all the time? Nobody dared ask that.

Tom felt that he should pose the obvious question. "Major, is your heart set on a male elephant? Or could a female elephant do just as well?"

Major Askwith nodded enthusiastically. "Indeed, another very good question. I think Schmidt can also consider that in his research." He coughed at this point and then continued. "I think it is true to say that we will want the least aggressive elephant. One that was assertive but not aggressive." Jane did her best to stifle some laughter. The Major glared at her and looked as if he was about to say something.

Luckily for her, at this point Bob woke up and decided to contribute to the meeting. Well, to be fair to him, he wasn't actually asleep, just quietly taking it all in. Because he was younger than any of them, he had this habit of putting up his hand in the meeting as if he was still in school. The Major, instead of addressing Jane, asked Bob what he had to say.

"Sir, I think we need to be sure that we source enough food for the elephant. We need to identify what we should feed it. What it likes and what it wouldn't like. We should try not to get a fussy eater. We should also try to get one in tiptop condition. Excuse me, are we also requisitioning this elephant? If so, they might try and palm us off with a pathetic one and keep the best for themselves."

"Bob, yes, very good. Yes, we need to consider all of this. I hope you're taking notes, Jane and Tom. Tiptop condition. That's what we need. A tiptop elephant!" The Major seemed very satisfied with this new phrase that Bob had come up with.

He turned back to address the meeting.

"Well, chaps and Jane. Is there anything else that we should consider, or should we set to work?"

"Where are we going to keep the elephant?" Clive asked.

"Oh, well, I've given that some thought. We're going to keep it in two places. We are going to have special quarters made for it. I have been given some plans to work with. We're going to get a carpenter in. Yes, I have to say, a lot of thought has gone into that already. The carpenter is coming from Elstree. I think he might bring a couple of guys with him."

"Isn't that a film studio?" Bob asked. They were all staring at the Major intently now. Was he actually going to explain what they were going to do?

"That is absolutely correct. It is a film studio and the carpenter used to work with a magician. Everything will have to be made in strict accordance with the plans that I have been given."

Jane thought she was beginning to get the drift of what might be happening. She asked, "And where will the prisoner be held?"

The Major coughed and answered, "Let's not go into that yet." He glanced around the room. "If that is all, I think we should get on with it." He picked up his papers and walked out of the room.

#

The Mansion house had its own library. It was full

of the books that the laird had stocked it with. Most of the time it was ignored, and the furniture was covered in dust sheets. The room was lined with shelves of books, as you would expect. The more valuable books were behind glass.

After the meeting, Jane and Tom went looking for Schmidt. They had been through the whole house but ignored the library. They were still unable to find him. They eventually went in there.

Schmidt had thrown the dust sheet off the table and was sitting at it with several volumes in front of him. Jane and Tom went up behind him and stood one on either side of the chair.

"Here you are!" Jane said.

Schmidt had been in a world of his own and seemed startled by the interruption. "Oh, you two. What do you want?"

"We just wanted to see how you're getting on with your elephant research."

"Not great, I have to say. I really should learn not to ask some of these questions in meetings. Have you noticed that whoever asks the question gets the job?" He didn't wait for a response. "Anyhow, as you would probably imagine, there's not a lot of information about elephants in this house. I haven't finished yet, but really the most informative stuff I have found so far is in *Encyclopaedia Britannica*. This isn't the most up-to-date edition either. It isn't exactly written for zookeepers, I can tell you. It would be helpful to know what this is really about. Well, it might be helpful. Or there again, it might not, because we might be about to do something really weird."

Jane and Tom cleared some of the dust sheets off the other chairs and sat down facing Schmidt. Jane spoke. "Whatever it is we're going to do is we can be sure it's going to be weird. The Major is being very secretive about this. Don't you wish he could just be open for a change?" She picked one of the volumes up and started flicking through it. Schmidt tried to continue with what he was working on.

"Aren't you more excited about having the prisoner to play with?" asked Tom.

"I suppose I should be thrilled. To take a former countryman of mine and really put him on the spot, asking loads of questions. Make him feel uncomfortable and desperate. Yes. I have to do it. It's my duty. I wouldn't say that I was excited about it, though. I'm guessing the Major will team me up with somebody. He's a cautious man. He will probably get them to help me know what to ask and then I will translate what the prisoner says. From the sound of it, there's a lot of high-level interest. Don't you think they're going to want transcripts of every interrogation?"

"Yes, but it's better than not having enough to do. I suspect that you will find it interesting once you start." Jane was a positive person. She liked to get those around her to be positive as well. She was actually looking forward to the challenge of finding the required animal.

Schmidt gave up trying to work and put down his pen and looked at them both. "I think you will have more fun with what you're going to do."

"You can come with me and Tom if you want. It might help with your research." Tom nodded at her suggestion. As far as he was concerned, the more the merrier.

"Okay, I will think about that. First of all, please help me with this. I don't have a clue what I'm going to say to the Major tomorrow."

Tom felt he was being too passive, so he chipped in. "Surely the main trick is to try and make it as convincing as possible. Or ask for some more time. Nearly everywhere is closed today. You can't exactly go anywhere and research anything."

"I suppose you're right. I haven't got much here." He looked down at the notes in front of him.

"Well, who would have thought we would be looking for an elephant in wartime?" Jane said. Then the two of them settled down to try and help Schmidt put something together.

#

The library became their private operations room. It had the advantage that nobody ever went there. They christened it OPS 2. It became a regular haunt for them over the period that they were stationed at the mansion. It was a secret place for Jane, Tom and Schmidt. The three of them made it a kind of private kingdom. It was undetected by the other members of the team. They did not question whether this was a good or bad thing. It did mean that at times they presented a peculiarly united front at the other meetings.

The morning after they had first found Schmidt in the library, the three of them met in order to discuss in detail how they would find an elephant in wartime Scotland.

They had been discussing the matter for at least 15 minutes and getting nowhere.

Jane said, "I know the Major said he wanted to rule out a zoo elephant. But don't you think it would be good to at least talk to the zoo because they might have a bit of a clue as to who is a private owner or who else might know about elephants in Scotland?" She fiddled listlessly with the pencil she had found in the desk in the corner.

Schmidt kept silent, but Tom answered, "Well, we don't even really have to tell him that we've done that, do we? He doesn't have to know that we went to the zoo. Unless we were to eventually get the elephant from there. If that is where we got the elephant from, he would see it on the requisition papers. That is, if he reads all his paperwork."

Schmidt just grunted. This sound was his total contribution as he was obviously engrossed in his own thoughts. He was, after all, supposed to be giving his report back to the meeting later that morning. He was trying to think how to fudge his way through it and what other way there could be.

"Well, maybe we should see whether Edinburgh or Glasgow has a zoo. Preferably one that's still open in wartime. I don't think I've heard anyone mention one. I hope there is one still open. If we can find one, then we should take a drive out there, you and me. If they will let us borrow the vehicle, of course. I don't see how we can do any harm doing that. I mean, we wouldn't be committing ourselves to anything. Maybe Schmidt could get answers about his choice of elephants as well." Jane turned to Schmidt and gave him a big nudge.

He kind of woke from his reverie. "Yes, of course that might work. At least I would feel as if I had some sort of expert opinion. I haven't found anything really helpful in this library."

"Would you want to come with us, or would you trust us to find out the information for you?"

"Do you know, I would really like to get out of this place for a bit. It gets all very much the same, doesn't it? Present company excluded," he laughed.

They discussed the mechanics of doing all this for a while. They would try to get the vehicle for tomorrow and, subject to the success of any phone calls, go off to the zoo. Jane thought that even if the zoo wasn't open to the public, it would still be staffed as the animals would need feeding. They wouldn't have just let them die because of the war.

#

The next morning, Jane made a few phone calls. She was able to set up that Edinburgh Zoo in Corstorphine, Edinburgh, would accept them as visitors. The animal population was largely unscathed by the war so far. The Major had given them permission to use a car on official business. He had also granted Schmidt a reprieve on his research until the following day.

It was seemingly going to be a bit like a school outing as Ivan the Terrible had done them all a packed lunch. They were only 10 minutes into the drive before Tom decided to investigate his package. To his surprise, he discovered he had Marmite sandwiches, an apple and some Scottish shortcake biscuits. He looked into the other packages and discovered that Jane had a superior lunch: she had been given a cheese and pickle sandwich, a Mars bar and two pieces of fruit. He decided to look at Schmidt's. He discovered that Schmidt had the same as him.

"Hey Jane, do you know why Ivan would give you a superior meal to ours?" he asked.

"Well, the answer is crushingly obvious to me."

"Oh, you mean because you're a woman?"

"No, that's not what I meant. Because I actually talk to him. Unlike you sulky men, I'm willing to let bygone be bygones. He was pretty frosty when I first arrived. I think somehow, though, I have managed to wear down his defences. For example, I bet you don't know anything about his family."

Tom got thoughtful. After a bit, she noticed he hadn't replied and asked, "Well, do you?"

"Of course, you're right. He is so annoying sometimes."

She laughed and said, "Oh, I forgot to mention I did ask for cheese and pickle sandwiches. Did you ask him for them?"

Tom stared out of the window for a while.

Schmidt took advantage of the silence. "Do either of you know when this prisoner is going to arrive? I have started to feel quite tense about the whole thing."

Neither Tom nor Jane knew when the prisoner would arrive. Jane asked, "But why would you feel tense about it?"

"Oh, I don't know. I think maybe it's just stupid anxiety. We spoke German at home and understood each other, but I wonder whether we were speaking a dialect. I don't suppose it matters that much. We used to make ourselves understood when we were still allowed to travel."

It took another hour at least before they arrived at the zoo. As instructed, they went to the tradesman's entrance. A security guard waved them through once he realised it was a military vehicle. Once they had parked, they went and found someone who could take them to the experts that they were due to meet. Unconsciously, they had expected to be shown to offices. But instead, they were taken to the elephant keeper. The man who guided them there explained that the same man looked after the rhinos and some of the other large animals. He said apologetically that his colleague was very busy and wasn't able to take a break. He hoped they didn't mind.

In fact, none of them minded at all as it was turning out to be quite a jolly day. They enjoyed seeing what parts of the zoo they could see from backstage, so to speak. Jane and Tom made it clear that they had delegated any speaking to Schmidt.

They were shown into a caged area at the back of the elephant house. Their guide left them there and went away with the mumbled assurance that somebody would be with them shortly. They look through the window of the door and could see that the keeper was still feeding the elephants. Schmidt observed, "These ones are quite big beasts, you know." They all peered through the window. "I'm not sure we're ready for any of that back at the base, you know?" They waited 10 minutes before the keeper was free to come to them.

"Good morning to the three of you. I'm Eric McDonald. How can I be of help this morning?"

Schmidt introduced himself and his two colleagues. "Eric. We need your help with a military matter. I'm afraid it is highly classified and I'm going to have to ask you to sign this piece of paper."

"What if I don't?"

Schmidt got flustered.

"Oh, come on now, I'm only joshing with you. Give me a pen and I'll sign it."

They then had to tell Eric the whole crazy story about why they needed an elephant. In fact, as they didn't really know why they needed an elephant, they elaborated and made-up some of the details in order to make it sound a bit more sensible. I mean, who would get an elephant if they didn't know what they wanted it for? Schmidt was able to get some of the answers that he needed. Eric McDonald was as helpful as he could be in the circumstances. To be fair to him, he had never had such a request before in his life. Usually, it would be the zoo who was trying to get animals from other people. For a while, he seemed to go into a stream of consciousness mode.

"Well, that is a very interesting request indeed. Are you sure you can't tell me more about what you actually want to do? You can't? So, let me think. Well, I suppose I could show you. There is no need to be frightened. They won't harm you if you're with me." The great thing about Eric was he didn't seem to require them to actually say anything back to him. They didn't have to lie to him much at all. He opened the door, and they went further into the elephant house. They could see that there was kind of a back alleyway between each of the sections. First of all, he walked them up and down. "In here we have the African elephants. If you look and try and estimate the height you can see they're pretty large. You say you're going to build something especially for your purpose. You need to take into account that you would need to build a much bigger structure to hold one of these. They're also strong *******. You wouldn't want them just pushing over what you built. Otherwise, you might be a flat little sausage on the other side of it." He winked at Jane. He seemed to think she would especially appreciate this joke. He didn't notice that she seemed indifferent.

"If you can, choose what is most practical. And if you are not hidebound by decisions from above, then let me show you the elephant that I think you should go for." He took them round the other side of the enclosure and then into it. "These Indian Elephants are my favourites. As you can see, they're much smaller. I find them easier to look after. How can I put this delicately? There is usually less to clear up each day, if you get my drift. I think they are a more handsome elephant as well. I think they're tamer around humans. But don't forget you're going to have to get it to do things. Come on now. Come and give them both a pat."

He insisted that they get nearer and touch the elephants. "They really aren't bad old beasts. We have never trained them to be ridden or anything. I don't think you could get anyone to easily ride an African elephant, although I believe some idiots have tried. But I believe in India you can actually go on an elephant safari. Well, I mean when there isn't a war on, of course. Well, you three, what do you think? Is this helpful?" They all nodded enthusiastically. Eric encouraged them to take their time and get close to both elephants. "Be careful that they don't step back on you. They're unlikely to do it deliberately, but they sometimes like to suddenly shift. Generally speaking, I never stand directly behind them. It just seems to make sense to me. Nobody ever told me that but, you know, I have heard stories about keepers getting into trouble."

Jane tried to broach with him the subject of whether or not one could be obtained from the zoo itself. "I'm pretty sure we wouldn't do that voluntarily. You can tell we've only got four elephants here in this enclosure. They're pretty hard to come by. Perhaps you might have less difficulty requisitioning them from a circus. Haha, how do I put this? The average circus has far less clout. The zoo has a fancy board with sirs and lords and stuff on it. But a circus wouldn't get on to a politician and start complaining about you. If I were you, I would start thinking like that. Think about circuses or private collections. By private collection I mean a home zoo that somebody's put together. I'm not sure how you would find those, though. We sometimes hear about them if something goes wrong and they contact us for advice. You know the sort of thing, when they discover their elephant is ill and they don't know what to do because they're amateurs. If the board asked me, I would resist giving one to you. You seem like very nice people, but you know, I don't know how you can get proper advice if you can't tell me what you're really going to do." He folded his arms and watched them for a while. They were enjoying being up close to the elephants.

"If anything went wrong you could contact me direct. I would do my best to help you. That's about all I can say at the moment, I think. I don't have a card or anything I can give you, but take my number. I'm certainly going to remember you," he joked.

He seemed to bring things to a natural close. They found him very interesting to deal with because he was helpful but without really requiring them to ask any questions at all. They each shook his hand enthusiastically, and he got his colleague to walk them to the entrance.

They sat in the car afterwards and had quite a long discussion. They agreed that they would try and find someone who had Indian elephants. They wanted something manageable if possible. All three of them felt that this task was turning into something that was going to be very challenging. They decided that it was a circus they were going to try next. But how would they find the circus?

CHAPTER 6
PIPPERFIELD'S CIRCUS

Fate must have been smiling sweetly on Jane and Tom. Although they stumbled a bit, their next steps in the search for the elephant were not that difficult to make.

Schmidt, Jane and Tom decided to go to a pub in Edinburgh on the way home. It just seemed like too good an opportunity to miss. A delicious piece of freedom to be grasped. Really, they knew that there was nothing to complain about in their circumstances. Most of their colleagues in the forces were having a much tougher time. They arrived in the evening before the pub got busy.

The three of them settled at a table that was near the front door. Everyone who came in would see them – perhaps that's why the table was still available when they arrived. Tom ordered three pints of bitter. There were a few old newspapers lying around on the side. Jane picked some up and flicked through them. She had no clear reason for doing this. It wasn't exactly boredom, but maybe just a pastime while Tom came back from the bar and Schmidt returned from the toilets. The paper that she was looking at was about a year old.

Tom returned before Schmidt did and sat down next to her. Once again, she sat startlingly close to him. She was almost touching him. Every now and then he would think about telling her that she was too close, but the trouble was, he enjoyed it. Why prevent something from happening if you enjoy it? She continued to flick through the newspaper. As was her wont, she gave a bit of a running commentary on what she was looking at. The paper didn't exactly have a fashion page but there was the usual goody-two-shoes advice about how to help the war effort and make the best out of your clothing ration coupons.

She turned the page and grabbed Tom's arm. "Look at this, Tom. It is brilliant! It's almost too good to be true."

There was a quarter-page advertisement in the paper:

"Pipperfield's Circus!
Come and enjoy the best
day of your summer!
We have clowns, trapeze artists,
jugglers, sword swallowers.
Don't miss all the live animal acts!
See our lions, the dancing horses
and our tame elephant!"

It gave a phone number and the location of what was last year's pitch in Edinburgh. Schmidt had returned at last. Jane grabbed him equally enthusiastically. "Look at this!"

Who knows what had just happened to Schmidt, because he seemed to have been struck by a sudden wave of doom. "That is last year's newspaper. They won't be there now! We need to get something more up to date. I don't know how we are going to do this."

"Don't be so miserable, man. Don't you see that if they were around last summer, they're bound to be back? Besides, there's a telephone number there."

#

The next day, Jane spent the whole morning on the phone. Pipperfield's Circus phone wasn't answered to begin with, so she had to repeatedly ring it. Eventually, she got through.

"Hello there. I'd like to speak to the circus owner."

"Who is this?"

She gave her name and rank.

"What's this about? We paid all our taxes. The Inland Revenue have been all over us." The man speaking to her had a bit of an Italian accent, or so she thought.

"No, no, it's not about your taxes."

"Did you say you wanted to book a taxi?"

"No, it's not about taxis." She started to get flustered. In the end, in her frustration, she gave the phone to Tom. Tom wasn't able to fare any better. After five minutes and not getting anywhere, Tom passed the phone to Schmidt.

After one minute, Schmidt was talking away in German to the other person. He became highly animated, and you wouldn't believe it was the same person who'd been so gloomy a few minutes ago. He put the phone down.

"That guy was German, you know. But he's been in the country since the 1920s. To begin with, I think he was a bit worried that we were going to arrest him. He was so relieved when I said we weren't that he became very helpful. The circus is at their winter quarters. He says they only really tour for three months nowadays. We can catch them at their winter quarters tomorrow if we choose to go."

#

Eventually, at about 10 o'clock in the morning, tired and a bit irritable with each other, they drove into a corralled area. It seemed that the circus was staying in a former factory. There was plenty of space to park vehicles undercover. There were all sorts of circus vehicles with brightly coloured signs on them, different shapes and sizes, some with cages that could be towed. They noticed this because, to begin with, there seemed to be nobody about. They wandered amongst the vehicles. They stood on running boards and looked inside cabs. Then, at the side of the building, they found a door. They knocked on it but got no answer.

"I can hear music coming from the other side. It sounds like a trombone," Schmidt said.

"I guess they can't hear us then," Jane said. She suggested they try shouting through the door.

"Come on then, let's just go in."

They went through the door and realised at once why nobody was answering. They could see 20 to 30 people there in the middle of rehearsals. There was a tightrope walker, tumblers and clowns. One of the clowns broke off from what he was practising and came over to them. They told the clown that they were expected.

"I will take you to Mr Pipperfield's office. Come with me."

They obediently followed as he weaved his way through various active circus folk then up some stairs to an office that had a glass window overlooking the entire room.

Pipperfield stood as they came into the room. It seemed to them as if he might be Italian although on the telephone, he had spoken German. He bowed to them in a theatrical way.

"Welcome, dear friends, to Pipperfield's Circus! I hope your journey wasn't too bothersome. What can I get you to drink? Is it too early for beer?" He didn't seem to need an answer to this question because he got a couple of large beer bottles out and carefully shared the contents between four glasses.

"Have a seat," he commanded. He fiddled with his moustache, which seemed to have been greased, and watched them as they all sat down. He waited for them to start.

Jane had elected herself leader. Maybe it befitted her, anyway. "We are approaching you about a matter of national security. We need your help with a secret project. We will ask you to sign the Official Secrets Act. You must not let it be known that we have approached you."

Pipperfield eyed them suspiciously. "Do go on. This is fascinating."

"We can't tell you why we need your help. We can't tell you what we're going to do with what we get off you. You mustn't even talk to your employees about this."

"I think I understand. You mean I should be all hushed up about what happens here today," he said with a gleam in his eye. He had a strong Italian accent and certain words were emphasised strangely. For example, he almost hissed "hushed up".

"We understand that you have two elephants as part of your circus; is that correct?"

"It is partly correct. We only have one elephant. It is young. The mother unfortunately died. It wasn't too long ago that that happened."

Jane coughed and cleared her throat. "I think we would like to have a look at this elephant now to see if it is suitable. Do you know its dimensions?"

"I don't think we've any record of its dimensions. I mean, we know how big it is because we train it." Pipperfield seemed amused and slightly excited at the suggestion. "Perhaps if you see it for yourself, you will realise it is a challenge I mean, which bit would you like to measure?" He chuckled happily at his own humour. He then stood up, beckoning in a theatrical way and marching out of the room without a backward glance. It appeared that he was used to being obeyed.

He took them through a side door, and they left the main compound.

"We keep some of the animals away from the main commotion. It is better living conditions for them. Some of them are like us and they need a bit of peace." He walked on a bit further until they came to another wall. He opened the door leading into the building, which was like a large garage and housed several parked vehicles. The vehicles had the markings of the circus on them. Each one was proudly emblazoned with the words "Pipperfield's Circus". Some of them were obviously custom-designed for animals.

"She may be sleeping. I suppose we will find out."

Jane was surprised. "Oh, a female." Tom and Schmidt, on the other hand, didn't seem to be paying attention as they were gazing around.

"Yes, what did you expect? Most performing elephants for the circus are female. It makes sense at all levels, the main one being that females are less aggressive than males."

"You appreciate we know very little about this."

"Yes, I regret to say it is obvious to me that you are amateurs. Yet you will be taking one of the prized possessions of Pipperfield's Circus away? I do hope you have a valid reason for all this and that you know what you're doing? She will need looking after, you know." He seemed to warm to his theme now, thinking perhaps that he could dissuade them. "Are you sure you guys really need her? Can you really tell me that this will help the war effort?"

They all noticed the change in tone, but only Jane felt she should say anything. "Yes, Mr Pipperfield, we ourselves have orders that have to be obeyed that come from a very senior place. Tell us more about her."

"Well, she can't be much more than four years old. We managed to get her before the war when we were touring Europe. We took a risk and brought a baby elephant. For us it was a risk because you don't necessarily always get one that is good at performing. She's a healthy little thing. Listen, is it definite you're going to take her?" He started to plead a little. "Surely there must be other travelling circuses you can try. Why have you picked us?"

None of the team wanted to own up to the fact that it was random chance they had found his circus.

Schmidt felt the desire to try and sugar-coat the pill a bit. "In our research, we found that you were the best circus around. Also, that you look after the animals the best." It was a lie, but Mr Pipperfield was unlikely to want to think otherwise.

"She needs her food regularly, otherwise she can get a little bit cranky. If you think of her as like a four-year-old child, then that will help you." He looked at them dubiously. "Actually, none of you look like parents. Let me explain. If you have young children, you will realise that sometimes they run out of energy. It can be in the middle of the afternoon, or in the middle of a long walk if you have forgotten to bring any fruit for them to eat. I want you to try and think of her like that. She will surprise you and want to eat, and far more than you expect. Be prepared to give her snacks, especially if she is working for you." He looked at Tom. "I see you are writing this down. That's good." Tom had indeed been scribbling in his little black notebook.

"I think we should see if she likes you. If she is going to be working for you, it's important that we introduce her to you. It would be unkind of us to let you just take her without any preparation. We better start with just one of you. Who wants to get in the cage with me first?"

The three of them seemed a bit nervous. Before they could come up with an answer, he had decided anyway. "I think we should try you first. Female to female." He put his hand out for Jane to hold. She had no choice, it seemed. In fact, none of them had a choice because he wanted all three of them to be introduced. "Here. Let me help you up the steps."

He led her to a trailer that was parked. It wasn't attached to any vehicle.

"But first, let me draw back this curtain." With a flourish, he pulled back a plush red curtain. Behind the bars, an elephant turned, looked at them and blinked. Without any of them knowing it, they had been standing extremely near to her.

"It is all right, my lovely. They are friends. You can trust them." The elephant gave a little snort. Could this signify discontent or disbelief? It was too early for them to understand anything about her. It could even signify contentment for all they knew.

Jane gave her hand to Mr Pipperfield. He helped her up the steps and pushed the cage door open.

"Come in, Jane. Elsa is a very lovely creature. You don't need to be afraid. Just stand still for a while and let her sniff you if she wants. It is her way of getting the measure of you. Hopefully, she will like your smell."

Tom, watching all this, thought to himself, "She will like her smell." He could see that Jane was trembling. It seemed that Mr Pipperfield had also noted this.

"My dear woman, there's nothing to be afraid of."

Elsa put her trunk out and started to gently prod Jane. And then, as well as prodding, she seemed to be sniffing – first of all Jane's clothing and then her face and hair.

"Put out your hand for her to explore."

Still trembling, Jane did this. The elephant tickled her hand. Her nose felt slightly cold and damp.

"I think she likes you. I'm quite sure that she has approved." The elephant explored both hands. Pipperfield added, "Try and relax a bit more. She can sense it if you are tense. Therefore, the more relaxed you are, the better. Now I want you to stroke her and pat her. But don't move suddenly. Aim to move confidently, but slowly. I want you to say reassuring things to her. Tell her how lovely she is."

Jane tried her best to obey this instruction. To those watching, it looked like she was really gingerly putting a hand out in order to pat the elephant. Inside her head, she thought she was losing it. She was convinced the elephant would panic.

Mr Pipperfield said reassuringly, "You're doing a grand job. Just keep going. Calm and measured moves are the best."

Jane felt the elephant's skin as she patted it. It wasn't like anything else she had ever felt before. It seemed so wrinkled and old on such a young thing.

"Hello, Elsa, I'm Jane. How are you today, girl?" She was slightly embarrassed because of the men watching her. It seemed odd to be addressing the elephant as if she were almost human.

"Stroke her more now and give her a little bit of scratching. Keep going. You're doing a grand job. Scratch her ears and lift her ears; for some reason, she seems to really like that being done to her. With animals, it's always best to do what they like. Especially when they're getting to know you. Once she is used to you, you can move around a bit more freely. Yes, that's good what you're doing. Scratch her ear a bit more vigorously. She really does like that." If the elephant had been a cat, she would have probably started purring. But elephants don't purr. She was making little grunting noises instead. Jane was thrilled that she was able to do this. She was bonding with the elephant. She wondered what Elsa thought as she looked into the elephant's dark eyes.

Tom and Schmidt gazed on with interest. Soon it would be their turn to go in the cage. For now, they were content to let Jane do all the hard work of being the first to make friends with the elephant. It was at least another 20 minutes before Jane was allowed to step out of the enclosure. Mr Pipperfield insisted that Tom and then Schmidt took their turns. The elephant related to each of them differently. It had seemed most accepting of Jane. Tom also seemed to go down well with it. Schmidt, by his own admission, was too tense. Elsa picked up on this. Although Mr Pipperfield was making them all go through the same familiarisation routine, poor Schmidt seemed to make the elephant tense. After close to two hours of this activity, it was announced that it was time to take a break for lunch. They were surprised at the circus troupe's kindness and hospitality. A group of the performers and Mr Pipperfield ate a simple lunch together with them. After that was finished, they were taken back up to the office.

"What do you think, tell me honestly: are you going to take my elephant away from me?"

Tom had been nominated for this part of the meeting. He spoke on behalf of the organisation. "I have to say she seems entirely suitable for what we want. We need to negotiate when we can take her. I am assuming that today is out of the question."

"Oh my. Oh no, no." Pipperfield adopted a very pleading tone of voice. "Surely not. You can't do this thing. How can you take her? She's our little treasure. No, you can't." Tom was sure that he could see tears appearing in the man's eyes. He even groaned and pressed his forehead onto the desk in front of him. "Oh my, oh my." Then he seemed to start praying in Italian.

"Sir, I'm very sorry, but we do have to persist with this. In this war, a lot of people have had to make a lot of very hard decisions." Tom instantly regretted his choice of words.

"Decision? This isn't my decision. I haven't chosen this. How dare you say that I have? That elephant has been under my care for a good long time. She has lacked nothing while I have looked after her. She's very dear to us. To all of us." He looked as if he was about to start screwing his clothing up and was wringing his hands in the most passionate way.

Tom was beginning to feel speechless. He did not know what to say that would help the situation. He uttered a few more things that just seemed like meaningless platitudes. He was relieved when Jane stood up and went to stand behind the old gentleman. She didn't try and persuade him at all. Instead, she spoke reassuringly to him. "It will be all right. We promise to look after her. I will see to it that she gets good care." Jane wasn't lying. She certainly did intend to do her best to look after the creature. Slowly, Mr Pipperfield calmed down.

It was, of course, impossible to take the elephant that day. They would, for example, have to negotiate about how she could be transported and learn how she should be fed. Towards the middle of the afternoon, they drove away. They had agreed that they would return soon to take Elsa away from where she was as happy as could be.

#

The journey back to base took place in a quiet and peaceful atmosphere. They were all thinking about what they had seen and experienced. As Major Askwith had not told them precisely what they were going to do with the elephant, they had unanswered questions. How could it possibly help the war effort to take this elephant away from where she was obviously quite content? This time Schmidt was driving, Jane was in the front seat next to him and Tom was in the back. Tom could see that Jane was just gazing out of the window a lot of the time, deep in her thoughts. He decided not to interrupt. Eventually, she spoke.

"She is quite a sweet little elephant, isn't she? Well, maybe not so little, when you think about it. I don't think you would want her to sit on you, would you? It was fairly amazing to stand so close to her, wasn't it?" Tom grunted and she continued. "I'm not sure we're really up to looking after her properly. What do you think, guys?"

Schmidt, who was concentrating on a difficult intersection, merely said, "I think you have a point there."

Tom had a different take on things, as usual. "I have been thinking. Do you think animals have a soul? Do you think they are intelligent? I just wonder whether they understand language, that's all."

Jane turned in her seat and looked at him. She said, "Well, you fool, that's about three questions in one. Didn't they teach you on the interrogation course to only ask one question at a time?"

"But this isn't an interrogation, miss!"

"Well, thinking about your last question first." She poked his knee playfully. "I think she could definitely understand Mr Pipperfield. And maybe even us, to a certain extent. I wonder whether our English sounded different to his English. He did have a rather thick accent, didn't he? Especially when you worked him up, Tom. Did you notice that he seemed more Italian at that point?" She didn't pause for an answer. "I don't know about intelligence. We used to have a cat and she seemed to understand what was going on sometimes. When I packed to leave for active service my mum insisted that she knew somehow that I was going to be away for a long time. My guess is they know more than we think they do. But at the same time, they don't know as much as us humans do. And as for a soul, what a daft question that is."

Tom, who had been afflicted with a feeling of guilt about taking the elephant, said, "I don't think it's a particularly daft thing to ask. I've been trying to think about the effect that we will have on her by transferring her somewhere unfamiliar."

"Maybe you should see a priest," Schmidt said. At first Tom thought he was being mocked. But Schmidt continued. "If you asked that in a confessional he would have to give you a serious answer. Mind you, it's not as though we've got a lot of choice about this, is it?" He became absorbed in his driving again.

Jane said, "I have never thought about whether an animal has a soul before. I have to say, Tom, you seem to come up with some amazing stuff. I don't know whether we could ever verify that as a definite scientific fact. It isn't something that's going to be very visible when you cut something open, is it? When it comes to it, we have to do this. Well, assuming they are happy with the elephant we have found. I'm sure they will be. There's not a lot of alternative, is there? Although I suppose there might be more than one elephant in Scotland." They fell silent again.

#

It was scheduled that they would brief the team the following morning. The conclusion might seem inevitable to them now, as they drove home, but of course these meetings could be hard to anticipate. They arrived home late and had a late night beer and some pickled onions together with some cheese sandwiches Ivan the Less Terrible had left out for them. Not much was said. There was a lot to be thought about.

Elsa, on the other hand, had a guilt-free evening and a good scratch on her belly from Mr Pipperfield. She liked it when he came to keep her company and especially when he sang snippets of Italian opera to her. He would sing passionately and sometimes weep copiously as he sang. This night of all nights he sang ferociously. She eventually became tired and laid down on her hay as he stood over her. He had taken off his black top hat and stood there in his red waistcoat waving the hat around expressively as she drifted into a long, contented sleep.

CHAPTER 7
THE ROOM

Tom woke early the next morning and decided to go for a walk before breakfast. The winter dawn had not quite arrived when he left the building by the back door and headed down to the woods where there was a footpath that led to a small lake. He knew from experience that this setting was invariably beautiful as the sun poked its shafts of light through from behind the trees. He stood still at the side of the lake for some time, allowing the early morning cold and sound to refresh him. Eventually, he looked at his watch and decided that he should head back to see what breakfast was on offer. He did not know what time the briefing would be but guessed that it was most likely to be quite soon after breakfast. He didn't like to retrace his steps, so he took a different route back to the house, allowing him to complete a kind of imperfect circle.

He approached the house from the side now, the opposite side to where they had parked the car late last night as they got home.

As he approached, he heard the cheerful

sound of whistling and of a hand saw being used. An elderly man in blue overalls was working away. Since Tom had last been on this side of the building, things had progressed.

He stood with his hands on his hips and took in the scene. An entire wooden room was being added to the end of the conservatory. Rather oddly, it looked like there would be no windows in the construction. In addition, he could see pulleys and counterweights. He tried to engage the carpenter in conversation. It began with an exchange which was harmless enough.

"Cold morning, isn't it?"

"Yes sir, that it is. Have you been around the lake?"

Tom nodded and ventured, "I like it this time in the morning. Good to see the waterfowl and everything." He waved his arm expansively and then thought he would continue. "You have made a lot of progress. It must only be three days. What are those cantilevers going to be used for?"

The carpenter's demeanour changed. Up until that point he had been cheerful and pleasant. But now he was cold and distant. "I am sorry, there is nothing I can say about that. You know, 'Careless Talk Costs Lives' and all that."

"But I work in the house."

"Then you should already know everything you need to know." The carpenter abruptly turned back to his work. Tom walked on towards the house and noted that the whistling had ceased.

He felt bad that he had asked anything. He should have known better, of course.

#

Major Askwith began the briefing on a serious note. He had made them all come straight from breakfast to the former ballroom that they used for most of their briefings.

"What you hear in this room you are not to repeat to anyone under any circumstance, is that understood?"

They all nodded or mumbled, so he continued with the briefing. "You have probably observed that the carpenter has been making good progress. You are not to speak to him under any circumstance." He turned and glared at Tom. "Yes, Tom, I'm aware that you have already tried to do so. The carpenter will be having extra help today because we have a deadline to meet. The German prisoner will be transferred here in two days' time. We need to be as ready as we can be for his reception. I plan that we should start interrogations as early as the morning after he arrives. Schmidt, I will see you separately about this." He stood up and paced around the room.

"Now I understand some progress was made yesterday with the elephant, and I want Jane to brief us as to what has gone on."

Jane rose to her feet, ready to speak to everyone. She felt this was a slightly redundant exercise as she had already chatted with most people about what had gone on. As she turned to face the room, she realised that they had a visitor and that it was therefore important to give an account of their journey to the circus and what they had found there. She went through the events of the previous day in some detail, but not so much as to drive everyone to boredom. All the time she was speaking, she could see the visitor peering at her intently. She wondered if he was going to be introduced to the room. She reasoned that he must have security clearance, otherwise he wouldn't be there. He looked to her as if he was a senior rank to the Major. She did her best to leave nothing out of the briefing. In fact, she felt that in order to be fair to Elsa, she should emphasise that she was a young elephant. Towards the end of her commentary, she departed from what she had intended to say. "We do wonder whether or not we should be looking for a more senior elephant. One that is more confident around humans and that is therefore more predictable." At this point, the visitor chose to speak. He did not bother introducing himself, and so they were none the wiser about his identity. It also became clear that the Major was not going to introduce him.

"I think it could suit our purposes very well if this elephant Elsa was immature." He seemed happy not to have eye contact with anyone in the room and continued to smooth the papers in front of him. "In fact, it could be to our advantage if she was extremely unpredictable."

Schmidt appeared a bit frustrated and put

his hand up. "Major, you still haven't explained what role the elephant has in this process. We did feel a bit hampered yesterday when we were at the circus because we weren't able to explain our true intentions to the owner. He was very helpful, but he could have been more helpful if we were able to tell him what our plans were."

The Major answered, "We don't want anyone to get wind of this. And I just want to say this will all become clear. Especially to you, Schmidt, at the first interrogation. I'm sure you will learn what our plan is. In fact, you three, Jane, Tom and Schmidt, I want you to liaise with the circus and take possession of the elephant as soon as possible. I imagine they will need us to produce some paperwork. So, you're to attend my office and we shall prepare it. I'm relying on the three of you to overcome any practicalities involved, which will of course involve feeding and looking after the living quarters."

It appeared the Major was hoping that if he kept saying these things often enough, they would just come about. Yes, in his head it was possible that a bunch of amateurs would appropriate and take care of an elephant in the next couple of days.

Alternatively, in Jane's head, a different plan was hatching. She felt that maybe it was too early to verbalise it. What if they persuaded the circus to provide a keeper? She wanted Elsa to be happy and looked after properly. She imagined that if they looked after her it would be chaotic. There would be arguments about whose turn it was to feed her. They would all feed her in different ways. In her brief encounter with the elephant, she had formed a sympathetic attachment. Jane felt that if they were going to do this crazy thing, they should do their best to look after it. The meeting finished with the Major's very definite pronouncement that they should get possession of the elephant as soon as possible.

As they left the room, Jane hissed at Tom and said, "Come with me. Get Schmidt on your way past as well. I want to have a quick chat before we go and see the Major about the documentation."

"Where?" Tom asked. She gave him a sort of withering look, as if anybody would know where. "Oh, the library." He answered his own question. He scuttled off to catch up with Schmidt, who protested. He thought he should be heading straight for the Major's office. Tom persuaded him that he could spare five minutes for Jane. Although, of course, he had no idea if it would be as short as five minutes.

Jane was pacing up and down the library when they entered it. "What took you so long?"

Schmidt looked at her and asked, "Why have you got a bonnet in your bee?"

"Idiot. That's not how you say it. It is bee in your bonnet. You know the bee that buzzes. Anyway, that's not why we're here." She drew a deep breath. "I want to talk through an idea I've had. I really think we should try to persuade Mr

Pipperfield to let us also have a keeper. I really think we would make a complete mess of looking after an animal. I mean, just look at us. Do any of us look as if we know what to do with livestock?"

"I think we would have to pay for that," Tom said.

She said, "Maybe, but don't you think it would be justifiable?"

At this point, Schmidt didn't even look like he was listening. He had got out his dictionary of idioms and had been trying to look up 'bee in a bonnet'. It turned out, though, that he could think about two things at once.

"Well, I have an idea, if you would like to listen to a suggestion. And if you aren't going to be smarty pants about my English. I think we might be able to persuade Mr Pipperfield to let us have a keeper. If you think about it, Elsa's keeper is going to be surplus to their needs if she comes to us. Don't you think we could put that to him? Something like we want to protect his investment. Protect his beloved animal. Why can't we have him? Or her?" he corrected himself. "What do you think? Does that sound as if it might be sensible?"

Jane and Tom stood up and clapped Schmidt on the shoulder. Tom said, "You might have something there, mate." He looked at the other two and then added, "I suggest we don't tell the Major at this stage. If we're successful, we will have a keeper and all we have got to do is give them board and lodgings. That is way less expensive than paying them a wage. He might even congratulate us."

Schmidt stood up as well. "Now that is agreed, I'm going off to see the Major. I'm already a few minutes late."

#

The Major was studying the plans for the room when Schmidt arrived. He didn't look up and waited for his colleague to come and stand next to him. Only the two of them were in the room.

"I really don't know about all this. It seems such a strange experiment to be running." He continued to gaze intently at the plans. "Still, if the Cabinet Office wants it, that's what they're going to get. Don't say anything until Tom and Jane have safely got the elephant. I don't want them to let anything slip to the circus guy." Schmidt nodded and then realised the Major wasn't even looking at him, so he mumbled his agreement.

"I want you to study this blueprint. Have a close look at it. It all seems a bit fanciful to me, frankly. They got somebody from the theatre to design it, for heaven's sake. You need to read all the small print at the side of the page as well as looking at the diagram. There are going to be some moving parts to deal with. The carpenter has been talking about cantilevers and such. It is all a bit beyond me. He tells me that he usually does stuff for the West End and even the occasional film at Elstree Studios. Anyway, it should all work once it's finished." He stood back to let Schmidt have a closer look.

Eventually, he sat down and started to fiddle with his pipe, but without lighting it. "Well, what do you think about it all?"

"I think it will be a bit clearer when we can see it full size. We'd better get the carpenter to demonstrate everything to us."

"Now, my man, tell me why I wanted to see you."

"I think it was about the German, sir. Oh, and of course the paperwork for the elephant, for the circus."

"I think that we will call him 'the prisoner'. We won't worry about saying his nationality. For security reasons, sometimes it's better to be vague. Everyone here will know he is German. At the moment he is being held at the West End Central Police Station. To begin with, the Cabinet Office thought that they might have a word with him. Then they saw sense and decided not to. It is always best not to give a prisoner an inflated sense of his own importance."

"How did they get him anyway? Was his plane shot down or something?"

"No, the truth is much more entertaining than that. He flew a small plane here himself, on his own. He tried landing it on an airfield but missed slightly. He doesn't seem to have done any damage, though. I mean to himself. It is our job to find out whether he is going to be an asset to us or whether he is in fact just a coward. When you interview him, one of us will be with you as a note taker." He paused, as if he was trying to work out what to say next.

Schmitz was shocked by the frankness of the next statement, though. "We have been told that we mustn't torture him. We have also been told that we must get the truth out of him. I think you and I and your colleagues are going to find the next few days very challenging."

They spent the next few minutes trying to get the paperwork ready for the circus. Although it was a standard requisition form, there were lots of free format entries to be made, so that it could be tailored towards their need.

The Major never lit his pipe and eventually left it in a stainless steel ashtray. He seemed content with the morning's work. It was possibly only the second time that Schmidt had had a one-to-one with him.

CHAPTER 8
BACK TO THE CIRCUS

Once again, it was the three of them that set off the next morning to Pipperfield's Circus to make off with the elephant so loved by all the circus folk, Elsa. What could possibly go wrong? Well, there was a reason the three of them needed the moral support of each other. Particularly as Mr Pipperfield didn't at this precise moment have a clue that their intentions were so immediate. Borrowing an elephant isn't like wearing your friend's suit for the night and then returning it. Or seeing what your friend's sofa looks like in your house. Besides all this, they might need two drivers to return, bringing the elephant with them. With all this urgency, they hadn't had time to think through the practicalities.

Elsa was happily oblivious to the impending changes and had eaten her fill and slept like a top. She had some happy dreams about Mr Pipperfield scratching her ear and calling her 'my dear'. He seemed such a nice man. At this point in her life, she really was the most contented elephant.

They must have arrived at the circus winter

quarters at close to 11:00. They parked in the same place and went into the building through the door they had used last time. What was at once clear was how quiet it was compared with the earlier visit.

"Where is everybody?" Tom spoke the question out loud that was on all their minds.

They walked around and took stock of the situation. The vehicles were all there, and the animals and the cages. But there was a remarkable absence of humans. At last, they found one caravan with evidence of occupation. They knocked on the door. Even though they knew there was somebody inside, there was no answer. Gently, they pushed the door open and peered inside. There was a man lying on the bed in full clown outfit. He was even still wearing his makeup, which was smudged. He was lying on his back, engrossed in a magazine. If you were to judge it by the cover, you would have thought he had bought it from a less-than-reputable newsagent.

Jane spoke first. "Hey, we've been trying to get your attention."

The man still did not answer. She moved further into the caravan. As soon as he saw her, he leapt off the bed, dropping his magazine on the floor. He did not speak, but a guttural sound came from his mouth. They tried asking him some questions, but he couldn't answer. He mimed to them, touching his ears and his mouth. At this moment, they guessed that he was deaf and mute.

They tried to mime their questions to him, but this seemed to frustrate him further. He gave them some paper and a pencil.

Tom wrote on the paper, 'Where is everybody?'

The man looked irritated and scribbled down, 'Church.'

"Oh my. It's blooming Sunday, isn't it?" The problem with living where they did was that they often totally forgot which day of the week it was. All three of them groaned at their mistake. Well, it wasn't really a mistake, it was just that it was a stupid day to try to do anything. Tom hastily wrote, 'When will they come back?' The clown wrote '1:00 p.m. or 2:00 p.m.' He signed at them, asking whether they wanted a drink. They said no. They kind of reversed their way out of the caravan, bowing to him and leaving him alone.

With three hours to kill before they could talk to anyone, they thought they would go and explore the nearest village. They thought about walking there and back but decided to take the car with them. Once they were in the village, they parked near the pub, which was called The Duck and the Orange. When they arrived, it was virtually empty. It was only just past 12:00. The landlord came over to them.

"It's not often we see strangers in this place. If you're eating here, I recommend that you take a table quite quickly."

Tom looked around, smirked and said, "Are

you expecting a crowd?"

The landlord didn't take offence. He merely said, "Just watch and learn. Where are you guys from anyway?" Jane told him a fairy story about them visiting her grandmother in the area. He looked at her sceptically. "I guess you can't tell me, then."

The pub was still empty, but they seated themselves at a table in the middle. There was a grandfather's clock at the side of the pub. It began to chime at 12:15. As if on cue, the entire pub flooded with people, clambering for seats and almost pushing each other out of the way. They glanced at the landlord, and he raised a glass to them as if to say 'I told you so'. They recognised a few of the faces as being from the circus. In fact, it happened that everyone was from there.

Pretty much last to enter was Mr Pipperfield. He noticed them almost at once and came over and grasped them on their shoulders. If he was unhappy to see them, he didn't show it.

"What a surprise to see you, today of all days. Don't you guys get a day off for Sunday? I hope you have some good news for me." He must have realised that almost the exact opposite was likely to be true. "Shall I sit with you, then?"

Jane pulled out a chair for him. She tried to be reassuring and was very much hoping that he wasn't going to be emotional like he was last time. Although, being from Scunthorpe, she wasn't particularly used to the Italian temperament. He made it very clear that eating was the first thing on his agenda.

"I don't know what that priest does, but I always come out of that church famished. Still, he's as regular as clockwork as far as his sermon is concerned. He is never a minute over 20. I think we should declare a truce until after the main is eaten. Do you three agree?" They nodded. They realised that the only way they were going to get anywhere with him was by coaxing him. Despite rationing, the landlord did quite a good job of a pub meal. Maybe in Scotland there were supplies that were of a more private nature. The meal was more austere than it would have been in the 1930s, but it was still adequate. The beer tasted a bit diluted. By this stage in the war, everyone knew not to comment and that acceptance was the way. They ate their main meal. They had some tinned fruit salad for pudding. And then came time to talk business.

Mr Pipperfield took the initiative. "I was really hoping you guys would change your mind. I can tell it's bad news, by the 'cut of your jib'. So, out with it, guys, tell me what you're going to do."

Schmidt, who was a bit more practised at negotiations, suggested that maybe they should go somewhere more private. He felt, quite rightly, that if they were in public, a scene might happen. But Mr Pipperfield was just as experienced. Now they were there in the pub, he was intent on taking matters forward there and then. But they had a trump card: national security, Schmidt explained

– they could hardly talk about something of national importance in a pub, particularly when Mr Pipperfield was being asked to keep everything secret. At last, they succeeded in moving him.

#

The next conversation took place back at the enclosure in Mr Pipperfield's own caravan. Tom, Jane and Schmidt already felt quite world weary by the time they got there. It weighed on them that they had a lot to negotiate and, what is more, if they were successful, they would then have to get the elephant all the way to the mansion. They certainly couldn't keep both Mr Pipperfield and Major Askwith happy. It seemed certain that by the end of the day, somebody was going to be upset with them. It was just a question of who.

It all started with a certain amount of civility, anyway. Mr Pipperfield and his wife offered them a cup of something and the five of them sat around the table. Mrs Pipperfield was very amiable, although she seemed to be there mainly as a witness and said virtually nothing throughout the whole meeting.

As it took place, the talk was a bit like a fencing match. There were thrusts and parries. One side would seem to say what they thought was a crushing point. It would, however, be countered with something equally challenging. Mr Pipperfield must have prepared himself well, sensing that there was not much he could really do about a requisition order.

It took about 20 minutes to get him to a stage of acceptance that the elephant was going to be taken away. Then, however, the focus changed to how that was going to be done in such a way that Elsa was inconvenienced as little as possible. He knew that his signature was going to be needed, but he also knew he could withhold it until he was happy with the arrangements. He kept saying to them, "I need to be very happy that she will be looked after." He paused, waiting for the others to consider whether this was a reasonable demand. Then he added, "When you have finished with her, I want her returned in good condition." To his surprise, everyone agreed to this aim very readily. Somehow, he had been thinking that the Special Operations Executive would be very relaxed about his creature. He realised that the three he had met might not be representative, but they certainly nodded enthusiastically.

Jane judged it to be the right time to ask him about the trailer. "We would like to take the trailer and some food with us." She sat back in her seat and waited for the response.

"I don't think you even know how you will feed poor Elsa. Maybe we will give you some food, and maybe we won't. Honestly, you guys are like a robber asking for help to take goods away." Jane genuinely couldn't work out whether he was being playful or contemptuous when he said this.

She knew that she had to ask the next question. It was inevitable and she had decided that it would be for the best. She cleared her throat and then said, "There is just one more thing that we want to ask you."

"Go on," he whispered impatiently.

"I think you will really see it's for the best. We want to ask if you could see your way clear to sending a keeper with the elephant. Someone to look after her and to see to her best interests."

He started to turn red with anger. His wife put out her hand and stroked his arm as if she wanted to somehow hold back the coming explosion. "Now I have really heard it all!" He stood up and looked as if he was going to hit the table. "You do realise you're taking away one of our star attractions? People come to our circus to see Elsa. They think she is wonderful, and you are going to take her away. But on top of that, now you want to take away one of the key acts!"

"We don't want to take an act away from you," Jane said desperately. She hoped that either Tom or Schmidt would join in. For the moment, it looked like this was very unlikely.

"Who do you think her keeper is, then?"

Jane stumbled over her words. "I really don't know who it would be. I assume one of the men. Don't you have somebody who looks after all the animals?"

Pipperfield was wringing his hands. "No, no, you're quite mistaken. Elsa is looked after by a Swiss female acrobat. She is called Princess Zelda. This is a very small circus, and everyone has to double up on jobs. If we didn't do that, we would never survive. We would never make any money." He looked at her with a sincere and serious face.

It seemed that they were at an impasse. It was at this point that Schmidt entered the conversation. "But she won't be touring until April or May, surely, and we still have much of January to go, don't we?"

He continued. "Why don't you lend us Princess Zelda for the moment? Just until we can get Elsa settled in and used to her new regime. I'm sure you could spare her for a couple of months at any rate. It would mean your elephant was better looked after. Why don't you discuss that with her?"

For reasons that would only become clear later, Mr Pipperfield looked like a little boy who was having a toy taken away from him. He then said, "Give us a few minutes. Why don't you go for a walk round the perimeter? I will go and talk to her. Come back in 20 minutes."

#

"Well, that is better. I think we're very nearly ready to roll." Jane straightened up, having hooked the trailer to the circus truck. It was just after midnight. She looked at Zelda and asked once again, "You really are sure that you know how to drive this thing?" Zelda didn't say anything in response but just looked at her very coolly. You could imagine that it meant that Jane was stupid to question her. Maybe it wasn't a very good start to a two-hour journey.

The afternoon had been by turns exasperating and entertaining. It took them a very long time to make progress. Now, at last, they were ready to roll and they had succeeded! Jane felt it was too early to give herself a pat on the back. They had first of all to get successfully back to base without any mishap. Mr Pipperfield had resisted for a long time and then eventually caved in. They knew that he had to acquiesce about the elephant because of the military requisition. But they had also persuaded him to loan them the trailer and to send Zelda with them to look after the elephant for the first few months. Jane secretly hoped that this would become a permanent arrangement. Of course, there was no guarantee of that.

Then, of course, once they had his agreement, they also had to get Zelda's. Nobody said any of it was going to be easy, but perhaps the hardest bit was when Zelda heard that Mr Pipperfield had decided on her behalf where she was going. Boy was she fiery when she was worked up.

"I am not zee piece of meat. That you can just decide that I go this way and that way. You horrible little man." She was most likely under 5 feet, but very fiery and so slender. She really got into Mr Pipperfield's face, wagging her finger and saying, "No, no and no! You think maybe that I am a fool? That I come from a nearby tree falling out banging my head and had no knowledge?"

Still, all of this gave Jane, Tom and Schmidt a wonderful opportunity to see the persuasive power of Mr Pipperfield in action.

Flattery was his first tactic. Compliment was heaped upon compliment. He actually ended up kneeling and appealing to her. Tom muttered quietly in Jane's ear, "That is one smarmy guy."

Next, he appealed to patriotism. Zelda was going to be helping the war effort. To listen to him, you would think she was going to stop the war in its tracks. A bit of flattery crept in here, of course. She would be regarded as a hero by the British people. They could see her resistance begin to melt at this point.

He brought all sorts of other reasoning into play. It would give Zelda a chance to see other bits of Scotland. Which of course was not exactly true because she would only see one bit of Scotland. She was promised the chance to meet the laird. They had to promise that they would make this happen.

So yes, eventually she did a complete about-face and agreed to go. She even seemed pleased at the prospect. Then, of course, she had to be helped to pack. They thanked God that only Zelda had to pack as Elsa was pretty much always ready for a move: she was kept in her trailer nearly all the time, except when she was practising her routine.

They were finally on the road by about half past midnight. They had decided they might need to swap vehicles regularly, so they were going to keep close together. Tom and Schmidt were in the lead in the small green military vehicle. Immediately behind them was a large truck with 'Pipperfield's Circus' emblazoned in large letters on the side. The truck was of course towing Elsa's cage. When the cage was in transit, there were curtains that could be lowered down at the sides so as not to alarm her. Zelda had to drive slowly and carefully. This necessity would hinder progress but there was no other way to transport this valuable cargo.

#

The high-value German prisoner was also in transit at the same time. It would not be easy to guess who would arrive first.

He was being treated as a VIP with regard to priority of travel, although not with much respect. He was afforded the relative comfort of coming up by train and car from his earlier place of captivity in London. It's interesting, as any other prisoner would have been thrown in the back of a prison van and bounced around on a wooden seat for a lengthy journey. The Prime Minister and the Cabinet were keeping an open mind as to exactly who he was and how he came to be in England in wartime. He had named himself as one of Hitler's senior aides. He claimed to have flown to England on his own in a fighter plane and to have landed that plane somewhere other than an airfield. They had found no documents with him. When they searched him, they found a wallet with a small amount of German currency, a picture of his dog, a smaller picture of a woman he said was his wife, and a minute picture of two children who may or may not be connected to him. If that was all there was about him, he might have been dismissed very easily at an early stage. Very little else of interest was found on his person when he was first searched. There was a particularly revolting handkerchief, some German biscuits, and a ticket which appeared to be for some dry cleaning that needed picking up in Berlin. There was a warning that if it was not picked up in time the dry cleaning would be disposed of.

The crucial thing that you should know about him is that he claimed to have hidden some documents when he arrived. He said to the first people to interrogate him that they were significant documents and that they could change the outcome of the war. The members of the Cabinet Office were torn between assuming the man was a fantasist and taking the matter no further or sending him for further interrogation. A couple of the more extreme members of the Cabinet advocated torture, while others pointed out it was banned by the Geneva Convention. It would not be wise, then, to create a precedent with this prisoner.

This is where the Special Operations Executive became involved. The SOE were aware that there had been a lot of money spent on AWE (Alternative Warfare Enterprise). Of course, this is what led to the secretive Christmas meetings with Major Askwith. The question that was repeatedly asked was, could you break a prisoner without torturing them? Eventually, a consensus was reached that they should see whether all the money they were spending on the AWE project was going to be of any use to them. So, rather playfully, they decided to set it up as a little game.

The prisoner would be dispatched at once to the SOE AWE project, who would be told nothing about this man other than the fact that he was German. He was to be interrogated at length, without the use of torture, of course. AWE was expected to find out everything there was to know about this man. This too would be verified. If the man never talked about any documents being hidden, then no further action was needed. A report of each interview was to be sent to the Cabinet Office. The time to be spent on the matter was to be totally open-ended. Major Askwith was warned that the project may finish at any time and without notice. The Cabinet Office would be the decision makers and would assess the validity of it.

CHAPTER 9

INTERROGATION 1

Schmidt had been summoned by Major Askwith to his office. He hurried down the corridor and passed Jane, who turned and asked, "Where are you going off to in such a rush?"

"To the Major. He has summoned me." He walked purposefully forward, not wanting to be distracted.

Jane laughed and yelled down the corridor to him, "Who is an important little sausage, then?" He did like her, but she could be a bit annoying sometimes. He wished that she was not so attractive because she flustered him. He thought that she must know that she had this effect on him.

He had not seen the prisoner yet. So far, there had been no briefing. Both Elsa and the prisoner had arrived on Monday. It was Thursday already and, as far as he knew, none of the team had seen the prisoner, although it was logical to suspect that the Major must have done, even though he was being very tight-lipped about the whole matter.

Elsa had caused a bit of a stir when she first arrived. They had tried to be discreet and hoped nobody in the village had seen them. When they arrived, the trailer and truck had temporarily been parked behind the house. It was shielded from sight by some hedges, and they had thrown a tarpaulin over the truck in order to hide the circus name.

First thing in the morning she could be a noisy little elephant, though. It seemed to be her way of signalling that she wanted some breakfast brought to her. She was still learning how to trumpet, how to work up a bit of volume to compete with other morning sounds. But she did not yet achieve the volume of an adult elephant. She would deliver little half snorts which sometimes sounded playful and at other times sounded angry.

The house was also not ready for the arrival of Zelda. She had created quite a stir from the first day. First of all, because there had been no warning of her arrival, there was no accommodation for her. Never tell an attractive Swiss woman that there is no room or bed for her! She was also worlds apart from the military mindset.

She stormed around, shouting. Interestingly, it had been Ivan the Terrible, the cook, who had been able to calm her down. This normally graceless man put on a charm offensive. He bowed to Zelda and said that he was sure there had been some dreadful mistake. He asked her if she would like a tour of the house and intimated that she would be able to select the bedroom of her choice. They returned an hour later when he had to start preparing lunch. She seemed a lot calmer. Up until now, the Major had been on a corridor of his own. Unfortunately for him, or perhaps fortunately, she had selected this as the most suitable location for her new quarters. Ivan had even promised her, as well as a bedroom, her own sitting room. There are other stories to tell about her, of course; for example, she needed somewhere to practise her act. She kept announcing, "I'm awfully worried I will be bored here." This would be accompanied by a very searching look to see if anyone was listening to her, as if she was expecting somehow that they should entertain her.

With all this in mind, Schmidt knocked on the Major's office door.

There was a grunt that he interpreted as 'come in'. He started to walk through the door frame and Zelda pushed past him. He could smell her perfume as she brushed against him. She said nothing and looked ahead. He shrugged as he entered the office.

"Good morning, sir."

The Major seemed to be trying to pick something up off the floor. He gave up and then waved to Schmidt to take a seat. Schmidt wasn't certain, but he felt that the Major was slightly flustered compared with his normal serenely confident demeanour.

"I expect you are wondering why you are here." Schmidt said nothing in reply, so he continued. "We're going to start the interrogations tomorrow, Friday. I thought it would be a good idea to have a word with you. I need to lay down some ground rules for what we do. Now, how do I put this? The Cabinet Office are quite particular about how we handle this prisoner. I don't think I need to emphasise how important it is that we do things their way. You are always to have somebody with you when you see the prisoner so that everything he says can be noted. Sometimes that might be me, but other times I would want you to use either Jane or Tom. I want you to impress upon them that they should try and make an exact a record as possible. These are to be typed up for the Cabinet Office."

"Oh, are the Cabinet Office going to be taking a close interest?"

The Major nodded and continued, "Yes, they are. Regrettably, I might even add. We're going to have to courier the meeting notes to them. This means that we can't afford to have much delay."

"Okay, sir. What do we know about him? And what do you want me to find out?"

The Major sighed and continued the briefing. "Well, Schmidt, this is going to be a bit of a challenge for you. I have been instructed to tell you precisely nothing about the prisoner. In fact, I've already broken that by telling you that he is German. It appears that our political masters want us to play a game. You are to find out absolutely everything about this man, but with no prior knowledge of who he is and what he is. I think it is safe to assume they want to know what he is doing in this country. Our purpose is to get him to talk. As the cliche goes, we want him to sing like a canary. And not just once. If necessary, we want to be able to write a book about him. In addition, my man, I think that you must work out whether you think he is telling the truth or not. If at any time he appears to be lying to you, then you should challenge it. Even if it seems to be about a small matter. Don't let him have control of the conversation, though. Only let him ramble on if you want him to. It is impossible to judge at this stage, but compulsive talking could be very annoying for you. You do want him to talk, but you want him to talk about things that may be of interest to us. I have known men who could fill silence for hours and talk about nothing of interest. I suppose we will find out tomorrow. Your target for tomorrow will be to speak to him for one hour. Only go beyond that one hour if it seems that what is being talked about is useful to us. You could concentrate mostly on questions about what he is doing here and why he came." He paused and then asked, "Is that clear?"

Schmidt nodded and said, "Mostly, sir."

"I have a question. You were with Tom and Jane on Sunday, weren't you?"

"Yes."

"Did you know before you set off that you were going to be bringing that woman Zelda back here with you?" The Major peered enquiringly at him and waited for the answer.

Schmidt felt slightly flustered – was he being asked to get Jane into trouble? He decided to be vague. "We didn't know anything about the woman until we got there."

"That will be all, then."

Schmidt got up to leave. As he did so, the Major said, "By the way, if he mentions the elephant, you're not to discuss it."

"Yes, but why on earth would he?" Schmidt muttered as he headed to find the others. The Major just about heard what Schmidt had said to himself and shouted after him. "I repeat, if he mentions the elephant, you are not to discuss it!"

#

Next to the prisoner's room, the carpenter had also made an interrogation room. It was a temporary structure that was made out of wood and had a corrugated roof. It was shaped like a large box. The walls, floor and ceiling were all painted a blinding white.

Jane and Schmidt entered and sat down behind a table. The table was standard War Office issue, made out of wood with a synthetic covering on the table surface. The only entrance to the room and the windows were facing them. On the other side of the table to them there was a chair which was where the prisoner would sit. Once seated, he would only be able to see them and the other three windowless walls. The intention was to disconcert the prisoner as much as possible. There was also no clock on display. The prisoner was not allowed to wear a watch, and although Schmidt had his own timepiece on, he told himself that he was not going to look at it.

Schmidt was more nervous than he felt he should be. Due to inexperience, he had been fretting about the interview with the prisoner. He had allowed himself to feel intimidated by the fact that everything was going to be written down. He had not seen the man himself yet and had not formed any opinion of him. The same was true of Jane. She was feeling much more self-confident, however. Schmidt's anxiety was mostly to do with performance. What was reported from these meetings would be read in high places. The Cabinet Office and the top brass would all be reading what had happened in his interrogation. Jane and Schmidt waited in silence until 9:00 a.m., when the prisoner was shown in by two guards with rifles. Throughout the interrogation, the two guards were to stand by the door, one on either side, so they could intervene if necessary.

The man did not look much at all. He walked towards the vacant chair. He was probably about 5 foot 8. Thin but not undernourished and wearing a pair of blue workman's overalls that had been issued to him. He looked like he had shaved but not taken much care over it. He was wearing a pair of wire-framed spectacles. He sat down and sighed.

Intentionally, Schmidt did not rush to start the meeting. After a suitably long pause, he asked the first question. He felt that he was about to climb a very high mountain.

"Wie heißen Sie?"

The man gave a heavy sigh once more and looked at Schmidt.

"What is a German doing here?" he asked.

"Wie heißen Sie?"

"You really don't need to worry about saying everything in German. I understand English very well and can speak it. Let us talk in English, and we will lapse into German if we have difficulties. What do you think about that?"

"What is your name?"

"I'm sure you must know already."

"My colleague is going to write down everything you say and your answers. For the record, we would like you to state your name."

The German looked frustrated. He looked backwards and forwards between Schmidt and Jane. "Which one of you is in charge?"

"I am," Schmidt said. Jane was writing everything down, although nothing important was being said at this stage.

"Trust my luck – how do you say it? My blooming luck. I have a German pedant boy in charge of me."

Schmidt tried not to look frustrated. He wondered whether the German had meant to say peasant boy rather than pedant boy. Either way, it was irrelevant. He felt the prisoner was going to be a game player. He asked again, "What is your name?"

"I am a very tired man, and I don't want to keep telling you my name. I have been telling everyone my name and nobody seems to remember it."

"Listen, then. For the record, I need your name on this interview. I need to record who you say you are. Let's just say it's for filing purposes. It's not a big deal, is it?"

"I wish to complain about my treatment here. I am not being kept under the conditions required by the Geneva Convention."

"We have no evidence that you are covered by the Geneva Convention. For all I know, you are a Scottish civilian."

For a moment, the man looked frustrated. Even as though he may have nothing more to say. Possibly even dejected, he stared at the floor. Then he looked up at Schmidt and Jane and said, "I suppose my manners are bad. I didn't sleep very well."

"Very well. Let's continue. We need to show for the record what your name is and where you are from. In fact, let's start off by you telling us your name and everything about your presence in this country."

"Gott im Himmel, it is beginning to look like I will have to play your stupid game. My name is

Victor Hoss." He went on to give a date of birth and a place of birth in Germany.

"Tell us what you are doing in this country."

"I flew here in December 1941. When I landed my plane, I gave myself up to the authorities. I have information that will be useful to the Cabinet." He sighed again. He seemed to like to do a lot of sighing. Hopefully he would stop after a bit because it was beginning to be annoying. He continued. "The Cabinet Office don't seem to want to talk to me. They keep making people like you talk to me. It is very annoying to talk to the bottom when I should be talking to the head. Perhaps you understand me?"

"Perhaps it all seems too vague to people," said Schmidt. "Where are these fancy documents that you talk about? Have you produced these to anyone? I think we should find out a lot more about you. Where would you like to start? Tell us, for example, what you did in the rest of December. I want you to tell us how you reached the decision to come to this country. How did you manage to get a plane and what airport did you take off from? I hope you're beginning to get the understanding that we need lots of information from you, not just vagueness. It seems to me that you have come to this country and you have been making bold statements, expecting people to believe you. I hope if you learn nothing else today, you will learn that you will have to give us a bit more information." He paused for breath.

Jane touched Schmidt's arm and said, "I'm having trouble keeping up with you. Can you talk a bit slower?"

"Maybe I could." He turned to the prisoner and addressed him. "Well, have you decided that you're going to tell us about December now? Let's make it easy for you. Let's start with the 1st of December and you tell us what went on that month that was so different that made you decide you were going to travel to our country and crash land your plane here."

"I am someone who could help your country a lot. You should understand that. Instead, you want to get outta me just trifling information. Is my identity of importance here? Or should you not be more excited about what I can tell you, the documents I can show you? It annoys me that you know nothing about me. Maybe that is just your little game, and in fact you do know everything that was told to the previous people."

Jane was struggling to get all this on paper. Her hand was beginning to cramp as she was writing. The Major had specifically told her not to talk to the prisoner, so she could not tell him to slow down. In frustration, she threw the pencil on the floor. Then, of course, she had to lean down and pick it up again. She swore as she did so.

This seemed to entertain the prisoner, who then enquired, "Tell me something. Why won't you let the beautiful woman speak to me?" He gave her a treacly stare. Jane felt uncomfortable. She realised that she could keep the rules that the Major had made by addressing Schmidt directly, as if she had a question for him. To make this approach very clear to Schmidt, she turned her whole body to directly face him.

"Schmidt, why do you think the prisoner is such an annoying little ****?" She felt no need to record this sentence on the notes of the interview.

The man in front of them appeared crestfallen at this event. Maybe he had thought he was being genuinely flattering to her. But, of course, that is not always clear to the recipient of the attention.

The words seemed to weaken the prisoner's resistance.

He slowly gave his full name, his rank and where he was stationed. Then he explained that at the beginning of December he had been living in Berlin, working at close quarters with Hitler. Note for editor. Is this the right city? He said would see the Fuhrer every day.

Schmidt needed to prompt him less than before. No longer was every piece of information prised out of him like somebody opening a tin can with a screwdriver. He was a married man and had two young children. He took pride in saying that both were blond and that he was the father of a girl and a boy. He said how excited his children had been about Christmas coming. Oh, it seemed like they could do nothing but talk about the presents they would receive. His wife had said that they were a couple of chatterboxes. He would work long days during the week. He said that the Fuhrer was a workaholic and that everyone on the staff had to keep the same hours as him. This meant that he didn't see the children as much as he would have liked.

Now that he had started to talk so much, they didn't like to stop him. But an hour and a half had passed since the beginning of the interrogation.

Schmidt said, "I think we will draw a line there and continue next time." He indicated to the guards to take the prisoner away.

Jane and Schmidt waited in silence while this took place. Then Schmidt turned to Jane and asked, "What do you think?"

"If he is genuine, I think he made a big mistake by not bringing his identity papers with him. It could be that they're hidden with his other documents that he was on about. You know the ones that are supposed to be so important to us. Don't you think if he is who he says he is that he would have wanted to prove it? What he says about the children is definitely true. And he might well work with the Fuhrer."

Schmidt nodded. "I don't know about you, but I'm tired now and I want to go and have a beer."

It would be a while before they could relax with a beer each, though, as they had of course to talk to the Major first.

#

Jane and Schmidt went to see the Major immediately after the interrogation. They quickly gave him a run through of how things had gone. He also read through the notes that Jane had made. He took a blue pencil and crossed some things out. Take this to my secretary. Get her to type it out on an official form. Jane was a bit bewildered that he had seen fit to censor some of it. It was as if the Major could read her unspoken questions.

"I have done that in order to make it clearer. They need to know he is pussyfooting around, and some of the things he said are meaningless and just add length to it. The Cabinet Office are capable of working out that he is being evasive." He turned to Schmidt and asked, "Did he mention anything that isn't recorded that there?"

"I don't know what you have in mind. But no, it is all there. Everything he said," Schmidt replied. He paused and then continued. "I assume you saw the bit about the Geneva Convention?"

"Yes."

Schmidt explained, "I don't plan to give that any room, unless we reach a stage where we have confirmed his identity. To my mind, it's a totally open question whether he is covered by the Geneva Convention. At the moment, for all we know, he could be somebody like me who has lived in this country for a while. But unlike me, he has walked out of obscurity to claim something fantastic in order to get notoriety."

"His living conditions are, let's say, basic, and perhaps a little unusual." The Major observed.

Schmidt looked at the Major but decided that he wasn't going to ask any questions at this stage. He felt that Major Askwith had an occasional desire to be very mysterious.

#

The prisoner was returned to his quarters. The room was painted a blinding white and had no windows. There were no tables or chairs. He did have bedding to sleep on: there was no mattress, but there were so many blankets that he was able to get comfortable with a bit of effort.

The elephant was still there. He was doing his best to not be frightened by her. At the moment, he was keeping as much of a distance as he could. This would inevitably mean that they did a kind of dance together. If Elsa became curious and walked towards him, he would walk away. If she was not satisfied by the distance and carried on walking towards him, he would have to walk down the other end of the room. She had been put in his room this morning. In fact, it had been done while he was asleep. She was too big to fit through the door, so he assumed that there must be some sort of other trapdoor mechanism that allowed her to be introduced to the room. She walked towards him as if she wanted to be patted. This provoked a period of about 15 to 20 minutes where they had to do their little dance. She walked towards him, and he walked away. He felt that she was slightly dissatisfied with him as she was giving little snorts. Against his better judgement, he found himself speaking to her for the first time.

"I think you want some affection. But I'm not prepared to give it yet. I never kiss on the first date."

Elsa seemed pleased that he had spoken to her and wanted to come closer. He inevitably moved away.

He was pleased that he had resisted mentioning her to his interviewer. Eventually, Elsa settled down. She stood alone at the other end of the room and just looked at him. He hoped that she didn't feel too rejected. He noticed that she blinked less often than a human would. In order to pass the time, he counted the seconds between blinks. He felt that he had become immersed in a battle of wills between himself and his captors. He looked around the room. He was convinced that they would have arranged it so that they could observe him. Glancing around now, he was unable to find any method by which they could do so. But they must have known that he was asleep when they put the elephant in the room. Time passed very slowly for him.

CHAPTER 10
INTERROGATION 2

Schmidt and Jane waited expectantly. There seemed to be some delay in delivering the prisoner to the room. Bear in mind that the prisoner's room and the interrogation room were only a few feet apart, so they could hear some sort of kerfuffle going on. It seemed that Hoss, or whatever his name was, was having to be coaxed to leave the room and join his interrogators. It couldn't be because he was too cosy. Eventually, the noise stopped.

The door was pushed open, and the prisoner was escorted in. He was held up by the arms, but only because he was resisting. He seemed to be strong and healthy but a bit dishevelled. Only 24 hours had passed since they last saw him. Today, he seemed less assured.

Schmidt braced himself for whatever was going to come next. He felt reasonably sure some more ******** was going to come his way. He was determined to be civil, however, and began as he intended to continue.

"Good morning."

He was greeted by a stream of German expletives.

"I think I can translate most of those for my colleague. Is that really what you want on the transcript for the Cabinet Office? Let's try this again, and you can be civil this time." He turned and dictated to Jane, "Good morning."

"There is nothing good about it. That elephant was snoring in my ear all night. I haven't slept a wink. What is more, she was doing these delicate little farts that didn't make much noise but smelt like billy-o."

"I'm sorry that you had a bad night. These things happen. I wonder..." He trailed off as he suddenly remembered the Major's injunction, repeated only that morning, that he should not talk about the elephant. He tried to stifle a laugh and continued, "I wonder what causes us to sleep well some nights and not so well other nights. I'm sorry you slept badly. But I think we need to start our business for the day."

"If this transcript is really going to the Cabinet Office, then I want it on there. What is the ******* elephant doing in my room? Why do I have to share my cell with an elephant?" He watched in dismay as Jane put down her pencil and did not write his outburst down.

Schmidt said, "I really hope you're going to be more cooperative than yesterday. It took us a long time to get anywhere. If you remember, you started to tell us about the start of December. You spent quite a time telling us about your children and your family and the anticipation of Christmas, but now we want to hear about what you were doing in Hitler's office in December."

The prisoner straightened himself up. For a moment or two, it looked like he had decided not to talk. He tidied his shirt. It had become loose, so he tucked it back in. Then he also checked the cuffs on his shirt and smoothed his hair down, as if he was trying to compose himself. Maybe he was even trying to find some dignity.

"I will not stand for this nonsense. I expect to be treated with respect. The respect any prisoner should be receiving." Jane wrote this down solemnly. He had spoken very slowly, as if he was trying to give her enough time to get all the words on the paper.

"Of course, sir," Schmidt said. He wondered if the prisoner was capable of picking up the slightly mocking tone. He decided not to proceed further, even though he was tempted to say something like 'is there anything else you want?' The challenge was resisted, and Schmidt returned to the refuge of his courtesy. "Perhaps you could continue to tell us about Hitler's office and what happened during the rest of December? We have really only just started. You have lots more to tell us."

At first, the subject seemed quite reluctant to say anything. But then he began to speak. He gradually became more and more informative.

It was then that Hoss started to give quite a credible explanation of his duties in Hitler's office. It seemed that he was one of several personal assistants that the Fuhrer had. His main role was to compile troop movements, both retrospectively and for future plans. He claimed that he had brought some of the future plans with him in the aeroplane and that these plans were hidden in the countryside somewhere near where he landed the plane. Schmidt made it very clear that he was interested in hearing the whole of this story. But Hoss seemed to want to prolong matters. It was, after all, about his only bargaining chip, and it could only be used as such if his story were true. For the moment, Schmidt allowed him some leeway in what he said. And so began a long digression about Christmas and the office party that was laid on. He was very taken with describing a woman he said was Hitler's mistress. He said that she had been involved in many of the arrangements for the party. Hoss was completely fascinated by her appearance. She was slender and blonde and everything an Aryan should be. He said it was very odd that Hitler had ended up with such a woman as she was not the sort that he thought should be with somebody in power. She was too flighty and a bit whimsical. He said he had repeatedly seen her with Hitler and the two of them were very close. He regretted in a way that he had felt he should fly to England before the party took place. He said that he would have liked to be, "on the wall like a fly to see all the goings on."

Jane wrote a message for Schmidt on a piece of paper. "Ask him more about his family. It seems weird how little he's said about them." Schmidt raised his eyebrow at her and then nodded. He was feeling frustrated with how vague some of what they had been told was. He thought there should be more detail.

"I want you to say more about your family."

The answer came back, "Is it not enough what I have said already?" To Schmidt, this seemed evasive again. But maybe there was a reason for it. He followed up with another question.

"What school did your children go to? Remind me of their names and tell me what school they went to."

The prisoner retorted, "Listen, you petty little sauerkraut. It is nothing to do with you where my children go to school or what their names are. I want them kept out of this. The same applies to my wife. The decision I made to come here is my responsibility, and mine alone."

Schmidt was not to be defeated. In an even tone, he replied to the prisoner's query. "I'm sorry to inform you that by coming to this country, you have involved your family and friends and a whole raft of other people. It seems naive of you to think otherwise. Your actions have an effect both in this country and in Germany. Do you really want me to point out why? In this country, they have an effect because we want to work out what you are really doing here and why. I imagine the biggest impact is going to be in your own country. There's no way I can put this kindly – you will be a suspect on both sides of the Channel. In Germany, you will be a suspect because you left and came to England, and your family will be in the frame because of that. Here, you are a suspect until we can work out whether we can believe what you're saying."

Whatever they were doing with this man meandered on for a while. Schmidt wondered whether he could even call it an interrogation. They hardly had the man frightened and trembling, with his back against the wall. But maybe that was old school as far as the Cabinet were concerned. They reached a point where Schmidt felt they had done enough skating around subjects for the day. He glanced at Jane and signalled for her to put her pencil down.

Schmidt's patience had worn thin, and he said, "Okay, you weird little man. We're going to put you back in your room now. When we see you next, I'm going to expect you to be a bit more forthcoming. You are definitely concealing something from us, and I don't just mean the phantom papers that you say you hid somewhere. I want you to have a long think about your approach to this. It will be better for you if you cooperate a bit more. Do you understand?"

Hoss looked a bit crestfallen. He mumbled, "Yes," then added, "I'll consult my new companion and ask her what she thinks."

"More ******* riddles!"

Without being asked, the prisoner got to his feet and waited for the guards to come over and collect him. He seemed a bit steadier than when he had first come in the room. The guards didn't need to touch him. In his head, Hoss thought that he was trying to leave with dignity. To Jane and Schmidt, it just appeared a bit overly dramatic, as if he was almost going to flounce from the room.

#

Back in the room, he started talking to himself. It was like a stream of his consciousness. It was all in German. Elsa formed the impression that he was talking to her. When he first returned to the room, she was on the other side. She had been quietly walking up and down in her new quarters. While the interrogation was going on, Zelda had taken her out and given her a wash. Then, minutes before Hoss returned to the room, Elsa had been re-introduced. The young elephant was a bit confused by everything that was going on. Now for her to hear German was a bit exciting. She walked towards Hoss, who cringed a bit as she came near to him. Somehow, he realised that her interest was not aggressive. So, instead of moving away like he had done previously, he stayed in position on the floor. She lowered her head and he realised that she wanted him to stroke her. At first, he resisted the idea of putting his hand on elephant flesh. He could not imagine what she would feel like. Also, he was a bit phobic about germs. Luckily for Elsa, she smelt quite clean because Zelda had given her quite a thorough wash, including a scrub behind the ears.

Gingerly, he put his hand out as Elsa offered the top of her head to him. He stroked that first. It really wasn't too bad. After a little bit, he decided that he liked it. To his surprise, he found himself beginning to croon to her. When he started, it sounded just like made-up songs. Then he unconsciously drifted into singing lullabies.

Unbeknownst to him, he was singing a trigger song to the elephant, one that her keeper used to sing to her when she was a baby. Nobody at the Special Operations Executive realised that she had been born in Germany. She was, in fact, a little German elephant! She had been conceived and born in captivity at Berlin Zoo. When she was a tiny wee thing, her keeper used to sing her exactly the same lullaby. Because of the circumstances of life in a zoo, she had bonded as much with the keeper as with her mother. Elsa was delighted to hear this song again. How beautiful and amazing it was for her to hear these magical words. Much as she loved Zelda, Zelda never sang anything like this. Zelda preferred to sing English songs. Before long, Hoss had a very happy little elephant on his hands. She decided that she was going to lay down next to him so that he could stroke her more.

When he saw what she was doing, he became a bit fearful because he thought she was going to fall on him. He was about to roll out of the way when he realised that she was going to let herself down gently to the floor. And there she was, lying next to him. She gazed into his face and blinked slowly. It was as if she was beseeching him, saying, "Sing to me more, sing to me more." The slow blinks continued. When she had started to position herself near to him, he had removed his hand from her. He realised now that he should start stroking her again.

He was fascinated by her ears. He put his hand out and ruffled the ear closest to him. They were all floppy, and it amused him. He found himself stroking the ear that was within reach and spreading it out. He started to sing the lullaby again. Elsa began to drift into a deep sleep. She dreamt that she was back in Germany. Her keeper was in the dream. This was the man who had first taught her tricks. In the dream, she remembered all the encouraging words that he would say, telling her in German that she had done well, that she was a good little elephant. In the dream, her mother elephant and her father elephant and her aunties were all there. This was very special to her because she felt like an orphan elephant in England. She had the company of all the circus folk, but that wasn't quite the same thing. Although she loved Zelda dearly, she could never replace family.

As for Hoss, he fell into the most relaxing sleep as well. In his slumber, his body relaxed. He kind of flopped over onto the elephant. Her body was like a little furnace throwing out heat onto him. Unintentionally and unpredictably, he had bonded with the elephant.

On the far side of the room, the peephole was open, and he was being watched. The aperture was not easy to spot. When it was closed, it was more or less invisible. If it was open, you could only really spot it if you knew it was there. The eye looked at him steadily at first and then looked round the room. The Major mumbled to himself, "Well, this is too damn cosy."

CHAPTER 11
ROOM WITHOUT A VIEW

The next morning, the Major called a meeting. He explained what he had seen through the peephole. In summing up, he said, "I think we need to disconcert the man more. We will make the days the interrogations happen more unpredictable. They will no longer be daily. I suggest that we have a pattern like two days and then miss a day and so on, and we will continue like that." He cleared his throat then continued, "During the resting periods when we're not interrogating, we will play around with the features of the room. I think he needs to be much more on edge than he is currently. As I said, when I observed him through the peephole yesterday, he looked as if he was…Well, how do I put it – far too comfortable? Schmidt, you have been doing a wonderful job and I think it's great. But in order to disconcert him more, I want to swap around who's interrogating him. Tom, you will also take a turn. We will definitely swap around between Jane, Tom and Schmidt. I may also take a turn as well. I hope all this is understood and clear."

Schmidt seemed a little perplexed by what the Major had said. "I hope you don't mind me saying, Major. You did say that you wanted him to be interrogated by a German speaker. What if he starts talking in German? Think about it – he could exploit the fact that Tom and Jane don't speak much German in order to delay things."

"Yes, that is what I thought originally. But clearly his English is very good. If he does start speaking German, just tell him what he says isn't going to go into the transcript. Although the Cabinet Office has said that they want us to take our time with the interrogation, I think we need to remember that there is a war on. Therefore we should try to bring it to a conclusion as well as we can. We do what we say. We will mess around with his mind a bit, but we will not be causing him harm. It is way gentler treatment than some we have dished out to prisoners in the past." He paused and looked around the room, trying to assess whether there was anything else that should be discussed. "Well, thank you very much. That will be all."

#

Hoss was pacing around the room when it happened. He was up the other end, opposite the door. Elsa seemed to think it was some sort of game, so she was pacing with him. Maybe this was something she did with Zelda. Maybe he was unintentionally giving the elephant a cue for one of her tricks. He would pace towards the wall and then turn around and come back towards the other. She would follow one pace behind and do exactly the same thing.

Suddenly, the floor began to move. He could hear that it sounded like a little motor working. The floor nearest the door started to drop. Where he was standing was rising. It got steep enough for him to start to slither down to the bottom. From his perspective, the floor was tilted at an annoying angle. Although he was slithering away, for some reason, the little elephant was able to stay in position for the moment. She stayed stationary as he eventually slid to the bottom. The floor stopped moving and seemed to reach the end of its possible tilt. Although he couldn't be sure of this. He lay where he ended up and moaned and then uttered some German expletives. He was very annoyed. As if to add to his feeling of injustice, he looked up towards the elephant and noticed her tail lift. The tail gave a little flick and stayed up in the air. Two balls of elephant dung fell out. They rolled lazily down the slope towards him taking divergent paths. To his irritation, one was heading straight for him, and he had to scramble out of the way.

The elephant took one step forward and suddenly gravity took hold of her. She very slowly also slithered towards the bottom, coming to rest next to him. Not at all perturbed by what had happened, she lazily moved her trunk around. The excrement was between her and her beloved. She had no qualms about trying to bat it out of the way using her trunk. That did not work particularly well, and it disintegrated.

For an hour or so, he lay like this. He watched the elephant, and she did not seem at all worried about the change in her circumstances.

He started to hear a commotion outside. There were angry voices and shouting. He could not hear what was being said. If he had been able to hear, he would have heard that it was Zelda and the Major. She was busy kicking off very dramatically. This was because the only problem with his little plan of spreading the interrogations out was that the elephant wasn't going to be fed. She was not going to allow that to happen. Things died down a bit, then went quiet.

The next things that happened was the door opened next to Hoss. Two guards bent down, grabbed his clothing and pulled him out of the room.

"It seems you're going for a little walk, man," one of them said to him. They made him walk between them as they did a circuit of the house.

When they came back, they just opened the door and shoved him through it. He stood still and looked around in wonder. The dirt was still on the floor, but the elephant had gone and the floor was level once more.

The door opened briefly, and Schmidt threw a notepad and pencil into the space before the prisoner...He spoke in German: "Write down your confession."

Hoss spent the rest of the day in solitude to contemplate what he had left behind. After a long time, he picked up the pad and pencil and went and sat against the wall.

#

He paused a long while and wrote slowly at first. He was trying to assess the effects of his actions. Was he making a big mistake by cooperating with Schmidt?

Even if he told them the truth, they might not believe him. It was certainly more fanciful than anything he had said to them so far. He sighed and began to write faster.

He didn't bother putting his name, rank or serial number. There seemed no point to any of that. He should, however, come clean as to what his real motivation was for coming to this country. This godforsaken country!

Here is what he wrote:

Here are the events that led to me coming to this country. This is all true, but you might not believe it. On the 12th of December I attended an early Christmas party. As I am one of Hitler's personal assistants, I was invited to attend his private party.

I was allowed to bring my wife. We arrived at about 7:30 in the evening. The party was in full swing. They must have been drinking somewhere else before the appointed time. All the Fuhrer's best mates were there. Himmler was being particularly obnoxious. He was singing some lewd drinking song. My wife is quite beautiful. The despicable man

Himmler spotted her as soon as she walked in the room. He carried on with his singing but seemed to be placing special emphasis on some words and directing them at her. I'm aware of how attractive she is and it is difficult for me to cope when men do this sort of thing. Particularly when they're a senior member of the Nazi Party. I used to be quite idealistic until I started working there. Then I realised that these are just men. They seem to be controlled by their priapic interests. Maybe one or two of them are okay. But there's a lot of rot in the senior Nazi Party. I'm pretty sure there is corruption. But there is also a decadent air about the place.

Adolf Hitler seemed to lap up Himmler's behaviour. I did my best to ignore it and went and poked around in the food, foraging for what I could find. I sensed I needed a full stomach. Who knows why? Then the dancing started. I have to confess, these guys know how to party. It was difficult to make sense of some of the women there. It was true that some were wives of soldiers and a couple were maybe wives of the Reichstag, party members... Then, in my view, there were some that were just prostitutes. Well, maybe all that is irrelevant, but perhaps not. The room was lit by candles. The Christmas tree looked magnificent. It was a tall one, decked out with all sorts of decorations. There was a band down one end of the room. Unfortunately, there was a lot of shadow. When I returned from the food table, I found Hitler talking to my wife. Eva Braun was standing next to him. He was flirting outrageously with my wife. But his woman didn't seem at all hurt by this and just started on me. I was doing my best to fend off her attention. Then Hitler kind of dragged me and his wife away. He pulled us to a side room then beckoned to my wife to come as well. He said something about wanting to show her his billiard table and his cue. I told him that I would join him in a minute. The fact of the matter was that my bladder was full and I needed to go to the toilet urgently. After I had finished, I returned to the main room. I crossed it and headed to what Hitler had said was the billiard room. I'm not sure I want to describe what I found in exact detail. The Fuhrer and Eva Braun were pulling at my wife's clothes. As you might imagine, she wasn't very pleased with that. She kept saying, "Leave me alone." That had little or no effect.

I was quite shocked by their behaviour. I had only worked in the private office for a year. You do observe things, but nothing too dreadful had happened so far. Maybe I overreacted or misread the situation, but it appeared to me that they were about to molest my wife quite thoroughly. I went over and pulled her away. Hitler wanted to persist, so I punched him on the nose.

Now, my wife is a strong woman, and not my property, of course. But even she was quite shocked by what was happening. When she saw that I had punched Hitler on the nose, she gasped. She hissed at me, "Oh my, you're in deep trouble now."

He stopped writing for a bit. He looked at the brown stuff and thought about the phrase '**** finds its own level'. He laughed and said to himself, "Or alternatively it rolls towards you and you have no option but to try and jump out of the way." He started scribbling again.

I was standing there gawping like a moron. Somehow, she had a better grasp of the situation, so she dragged me from the room. As we left and closed the door, we could hear Hitler moaning. We assumed it might be a little while before he got a grip of himself. Surely nobody had dared to punch the Fuhrer on the nose ever before. I told her to go ahead and wait near where the car was parked.

Meanwhile, I hurried down the corridor towards the private office. I was intent on revenge, so I scurried around in the troop movements folders. I tried to select what would be most to my advantage. Yes, I admit it I was intent on revenge at the time. When I had been in the Hitler Youth, I was enthusiastic and besotted – as most of us were. My year in the private office had shown me that he had feet of clay. I left the office grasping two cardboard tubes. They are what I fled the country with. I have hidden the tubes where I think nobody will find them.

Nobody questioned me as I left the chancery. It was semi-normal for me to be walking around late at night. The cardboard tubes might have given some interest to the guards, but they didn't want to stop me. Maybe they were feeling too idle. I could, of course, have been making a good effort at looking nonchalant. Something makes me doubt that, however.

I went and found my wife. She was waiting near the car but standing in the shadows in the hope that nobody would see her. We got in and drove off. She started at once, "They're going to hunt you down and kill you. You know exactly what they are like. Where can you go that you will be safe? The children and I can join you later."

Before the war, I had trained as a pilot. I told her my plan. It was put together in haste and it was very stupid. I can tell that from the reception you have given me. You probably won't even believe me now. I'm here for revenge on Hitler. I'm sick with worry about my family and I know they can't come to the country right now. But I'm willing to trade my cooperation if after the war you would help them to do so. If you make that promise, I will show you where the plans are hidden.

He put the paper down. He was leaning against the wall with his feet out in front of him, staring into the whiteness of the room. Now that he had written all that, he was contemplating tearing it up and not handing it over. Schmidt might not believe him. Maybe that woman would. Right now, he was feeling despair at what he had done.

Suddenly the whole of the right-hand wall lowered outward on a hinge. He could see the trees and greenery of the outside world. He had not seen that since he had arrived at this strange place. He saw a woman dressed in a circus acrobat costume. It was Zelda, but of course he did not know that.

She bent down and put some hessian sacking on the lowered wall. She clapped her hands and Elsa trotted over and walked across the hessian and into the room. Zelda bowed and blew him a kiss playfully. He thought to himself, "That is how they get her in and out!" Elsa came over to him and lowered her head for him to give her some attention. As she did so, the wall behind her rose from the ground and sealed the room off once more, leaving the prisoner with the elephant for company.

CHAPTER 12
BREAKING POINT

The night-time wanderings of the Major and Zelda were raising suspicion amongst the team members. Whenever they discussed the matter, opinion was divided into two camps. There were those that thought there was a legitimate excuse for all the wanderings around the house. It could be, for example, that Zelda had something that she needed to do with the elephant. Perhaps she was afraid of the dark and needed the Major's special help. And there were those who thought the opposite, that Zelda didn't worry at all about the elephant in the night. She had needs of a much more primeval nature and had alighted on the Major's physique as a way of satisfying these. For someone in his fifties, he was a handsome devil and could be seen to be quite a catch for a certain sort of lithe Swiss nymphomaniac. Nothing was known of his family circumstances. It was not known whether he was married or had a family. He was such a secretive little bunny that nobody even knew where he was from. He had spent so long in SOE that he had developed an attitude of permanent secrecy.

Today's particular wandering started at 5:00 a.m. If anyone had been on the corridor that Zelda and the Major slept on, they would have seen him coming out of his room and going and knocking on her door. Today they had an assignment rather than an assignation. Hoss's written confession or statement was yet to be read; it was still in the room. Today, at this early time in the morning, the Major was intent on using a feature of the room that had not been activated so far. Zelda was along for the ride because she needed to observe through the peephole in order to take care of the elephant.

Hoss was lying on the floor on his blankets. He had still not earned the privilege of a bed. Elsa was lying near him and throwing off her body odour and the occasional sigh in her sleep. Who knew where she was in her dreams this time? He was awake. He had not had a good night and he was lying on his back with a good view of the ceiling.

The peephole opened and Zelda looked through it. She could just about make out the shape of the man lying there on his blankets. She shouted to the Major, "It's okay, you can start the machinery now. The elephant is lying down."

The Major pushed the button and pulled the lever. There was a sudden shudder as the motors began to work.

Hoss double-blinked in shock. The walls were beginning to move! The wall that was nearest to him was stationary, but two of the other walls were definitely moving. He couldn't believe his eyes to begin with. He could hear the motor chugging as the walls moved towards him. In bewilderment, he stared as two of the walls moved. He jumped to his feet and started swearing in German. He was jumping up and down and waving his clenched fist. Elsa didn't like this and rose to her feet. She didn't like leaving her dreamy deep sleep so quickly. She wondered what was wrong with the human and why he was so upset. He had been so cosy last night. What was making him bounce up and down in anger? She did not like being around angry people. She raised her trunk and trumpeted at him. The noise of this so near to his ear was quite deafening.

Zelda shouted to the Major to stop for a moment. The room had reduced to half its size.

"I want to go further, Zelda. He needs to feel uncomfortable."

"If you hurt my little elephant, you'll be in deep trouble. You will be the one feeling uncomfortable, I can assure you. Be patient now and wait. Let the two of them settle down a bit."

It was five minutes before she gave the instruction to start again. The two moveable walls shrank the room further.

"Enough, enough!" she said. "That's too much! If you make Elsa too uncomfortable, she may attack him."

Hoss was groaning in disbelief. He wasn't

quite being squashed by the elephant, but he was very close to it. Zelda had resisted the urge to let the Major push them closer together. It wasn't Hoss that she was worried about, it was dear Elsa. The prisoner, meanwhile, was mumbling and grumbling something rotten. The space he was occupying was now a quarter of the original size of the room. He wanted to pace around and mutter, but actually, that wasn't possible. He could stand up but could only take one pace in each direction. If he went one way, he would go straight into the wall, and of course it wouldn't make sense to do that. If he paced the other way, he would walk into Elsa. The way she was currently positioned, he would walk into her posterior. Much as he liked her, he didn't want to do this. If Elsa shifted round, he would hit a different part of her body. He started to shout.

"What do you think you're doing, you morons? This isn't fair to either of us."

It was useless to speak because the Major and Zelda had gone off together for a morning walk. Maybe there was some truth in the rumours after all.

It was a while before Hoss realised that all his protests were futile. The elephant seemed restless as well and slowly shifted her position so that she could face him. Her eyes looked into his and she was blinking and going slightly cross-eyed. He did not think that she was trying to communicate anything to him other than distress.

Then she shifted around again and pushed her rear into him. He pushed his way through until he was at her side. She kept waving her trunk upwards, as if she was wanting him to look where she was pointing. He thought it must be his imagination, but she did seem very insistent about this. Eventually, the penny dropped and he realised that she was gesturing towards a glimpse of sky. It was just a tiny white strip at the top.

He stroked her ears and said, "I think you're trying to tell me things are not as bad as they look. Do you think we can make the wall drop away together?" He ruffled her ear in just the way she liked. He wanted to try and climb on her back. She didn't like that at all and wasn't cooperating with him. He found himself saying to her, "If only you could go on your hind legs like you do for your tricks." He knew she wasn't happy, so he started singing the German lullaby to her again.

He did not know what sparked the action, but she gradually went on to her hind legs. Hesitatingly, she took a couple of steps forward. She rested her forelegs against the wall. Then she started to tap and beat the wall. Hoss became very excited. He started to shout encouragement to her. It was in German, but translated it was very simple. He said over and over, "Good girl! Well done!"

There was now a dreadful creaking and cracking noise. The side of the room suddenly started to give way. Because this was the side they had introduced the elephant from, there was a giant hinge at the bottom next to the floor. Elsa was somehow making this go down. It didn't go all the way and got stuck; however, the gap was big enough for them both to get through. The elephant and the German were both liberated. Hoss took one look at her and wondered if they should both go the same way. Reaching a decision, he said, "Elsa, you stay here, darling. You mustn't come with me." He patted her trunk lovingly. She tried to fold her trunk around his wrist. He shook it free. He gave another quick pat to her trunk and then began to run.

Elsa started after him but wasn't able to keep up. It didn't take long for him to disappear into the bushes. She followed him through the same gap and was already lagging far behind.

Because he had arrived by car, he didn't really know anything at all about the site. For example, he was unaware that his room, his dazzling white room, was situated next to this ancient mansion. Once through the bushes he found himself in a leafy glade. He really didn't have a clue which direction to go in. He felt that he had no choice other than to select at random. So he burst into another wooded area. This time everything was a bit denser, but then he could see a path. He was running on ahead and she was coming along far behind him. She was panting and then she did a loud trumpet. He stopped and turned round and shushed her. "No noise, my

Liebling." Then he started running again, and she did her best to trail him.

#

Meanwhile, the Major and Zelda were having their walk in the woods as well. Fortunately for the prisoner, they were the other side of the mansion. The rumours were true. They were walking hand in hand through the woods. Something was going on, but not necessarily what everyone thought – well, for the moment, at any rate, things were perfectly non-sexual.

As they were walking, they were having a solemn conversation about what they would do after the war. It was Zelda who had introduced the subject. She had done it in the hope that she would get some sort of statement of commitment out of her circumspect companion.

"I like to think where I can go after the war. I am finding Scotland very nice. It is a beautiful part of the country. Maybe I would like to go to an island just off the coast. Get a little crofter's cottage. What do you think? Is that a nice idea?"

The Major stared at the ground thoughtfully. They continued to walk and then he spoke. "I haven't given it much thought myself. I do hope it is a war that has an ending." He realised that this was maybe a bit negative for Zelda, so he tried to adopt a more positive approach. He squeezed her hand and said, "of course it must finish. To be on an island might be nice, but it might get lonely. I would quite like to be where there's a lot of people, so London would be appealing. I could get a job in one of the banks or something?"

Zelda was not to be defeated so easily. She felt a little tweak of anger that he had not picked up on her hint, although she was learning that it was quite normal for him to be like this. She started to mount a counteroffensive. "Of course, only one other person is needed to cure loneliness. If I was on the island, I know a nice man who would stop me from being lonely and who would keep me warm at nights." She glanced at him to see whether he was getting the picture. She was relieved because it appeared that he did. But just as quickly, her hopes were dashed again as he started to speak.

"Oh, you mean you would get your brother to come and help you on the croft?" He said this in all innocence, as he really had very little experience with women. Since a bad experiment in adolescence, he had kept his distance from them and lived a non-sexual life. He had found his secretive profession quite to his liking. It was only with the arrival of Zelda that his eyes had been opened and his sexual life had started like a floodgate. He was both intrigued and worried by turns. She had a kind of molten temperament that would flick backwards and forwards between indifference and torrid passion. He looked at her happily but then realised that she was on the verge of an explosion. He must have done something wrong or said something wrong, he thought to himself. He also thought, "Here we go again."

She hit him and exclaimed, "Not my brother, you stinking fool. You would be the cure for my loneliness. You and your handsome body. You could help me by ploughing my furrow."

She had stopped and was facing him on the path.

He stuttered and said, "I think you will find you need more than one thorough plough to make any difference if you're going to try and be self-sustaining." She gave him a gentle punch.

"You silly man. That isn't the kind of furrow that I was thinking about." She ran her index finger softly down the fly on his trousers. She was contemplating unzipping him.

She put her hand out thoughtfully and traced the edge of his trouser flies gently with her index finger. She was deep in thought.

At this moment, Bob and Clive came running down the path towards them. Bob clearly saw what she was about to do, but Clive didn't.

Zelda looked disappointed, as if a plate of food had been suddenly taken away from her.

Clive spoke first. He was out of breath from the running and so panted, "Sir, I am sorry to bother you both. The prisoner and the elephant have got out. We're not sure which way they have gone. I thought you would want to know as soon as possible."

The Major spoke to himself more than

anyone else, saying, "How the hell did that happen?"

Bob said, "Somehow, he managed to get the room wall down on one side. The one with the hinge. It is kind of stuck halfway down and he managed to get himself and the elephant out."

The Major started to walk. "Oh, damn. Well, come on, we'd better get back to the house." He broke into a run. The enormity of the situation hit him. This wasn't just any prisoner. The Cabinet Office were intensely interested. He couldn't bear the thought of what effect it would have on his career.

The four of them ran along the path back to the room and to the mansion. It was still quite early, well before breakfast.

Once they arrived at the house, he instructed them. "Go and find everyone. Get them to the kitchen. If they're still asleep, make sure they get up quickly. Zelda, you come with me and let's have a quick look at that room together."

They went and stood in the room. He observed to her, "I don't know how bust it is, but it was obviously making it smaller that did that." He hit the side of the wall. "I should have stopped where you told me to. It would have probably been enough."

Zelda was wringing her hands in anguish. "I don't care about that stupid man," she said. "I'm worried about my little Elsa. If anyone hurts that elephant, they will be in trouble."

The Major did his best to look as if he cared about the elephant. He knew enough to know that he should. He asked her, "Do you think she would go off on her own or would she follow him?"

She looked imploringly at him. "You've got to find my sweet, you've got to find her. I think she will follow him. She will probably go anywhere he goes." Then she started sobbing. "It will be better if she is with him. I can't bear the thought of her blundering around on her own. It would be really dreadful. She would feel so lonely. She has always been in captivity."

The Major, of course, was much more worried about getting the prisoner back. He wouldn't say this to Zelda, but it would be far less concerning to him if he had lost the elephant but not the prisoner. She was trying to get him to hug her. He, for his part, wanted to impress upon her a sense of urgency.

"Come on now, we must away to the kitchen. The sooner we set out, the sooner we will find them."

As he walked out of the room, he kicked the notebook that Hoss had been writing in. He was surprised to see it on the floor. He bent down and picked it up. He flipped through it and realised what it was – some sort of confession written in pencil.

When they got to the kitchen, everyone was there, including Ivan the Terrible. As soon as he saw them, he asked, "Well, do I do breakfast for everyone or not?"

Impulsively, the Major answered, "No, everyone is to go out at once. Start searching. Go in pairs. But first, let us think where the prisoner might go. Schmidt, do you have any thoughts? Any insights into what he might do would be helpful. It appears that he was writing a confession yesterday, Schmidt. What do you know about that?"

"Well, I asked him to do it. I haven't seen it yet. Maybe we should read it through first? How long is it?"

The Major handed Schmidt the notebook and mumbled, "Go on, then. Read it out. It won't take long. Everyone should hear it. If you have any thoughts, say them."

Schmidt read it all out loud. There was a pause.

And then Tom said, "He might go and try to find the documents that he says he hid. If he decides to do that, he will probably not travel with the elephant. She will be too slow compared with him. Plus, she will attract the attention of the local constabulary. We need to issue an alert to the police so they can keep an eye out for an elephant." The humour struck him, but he was trying to restrain himself. "We need to tell them that if they see an elephant, they should contact us. They should do it without delay and let us know the coordinates."

Zelda started weeping copiously at the

thought of Elsa being on her own. Jane went over to her and hugged her. She whispered in her ear, "It will be all right. We will get her back, don't worry."

The Major was worried about all this emotion. "Right then, action stations. Everyone get out there and find them. Schmidt, stay with me a minute or two." He handed Schmidt the notebook and said, "Get everything in here typed up as soon as you can. Then when we get back, we can read through it and work out what we're going to do with it."

"Sir, do you think we should let the Cabinet Office know what has happened?"

The Major stared at him incredulously. "No, definitely not. We will wait until we get the man back. And only then will we work out whether we bother telling them!"

CHAPTER 13
THE CHASE

The ensuing chase was not a great credit to British intelligence. They left the mansion in pairs but had not thought about how they would keep each other updated. In addition, they had left no one at base except for Ivan the cook. Unfortunately, he was the sort of person who was happily oblivious to contact with the outside world. His domain was in the kitchen and that was where he stayed. Even on a normal day, he would never answer the phone. His aversion to telephone communications extended further on days when there were special emergencies.

As might be expected, Tom and Jane left together. Although they weren't an item, they were always doing things as a twosome. They decided to search the grounds of the mansion using bicycles. The grounds were extensive; they spread out a long way and there were many footpaths. In some places, there were no footpaths at all. They felt it would take the prisoner quite a long time to find his way out of the grounds, particularly as he was not familiar with them.

Clive and Bob teamed up. They took the car that the team used. Their intention was to drive around the local roads and to go to the local villages to see whether anyone mentioned any unusual behaviour.

Zelda and Major Askwith left together. Of course, Zelda was not SOE personnel. Well, not officially, but she was certainly motivated to find what she referred to as "zee darling little elephant." The fact of the matter was she was indifferent to whether or not the German was recovered. She had a bit of antipathy towards that country and its inhabitants. She was capable of being polite to Hoss. That was about all.

The Major was a bit miffed to find that the car had already gone. He and Zelda therefore had sloppy seconds in the sense that they had to use the truck. He was not used to driving it and found it a bit awkward. After five minutes of enduring this, Zelda ordered him out of the driving seat.

She bossed him about, saying, "Let me drive. You don't seem to know how to change gear."

He wasn't exactly meek when he got out of the truck. He muttered furiously, "I suppose you are so much better." He got in on the passenger side and slammed the door rather emphatically. They had the same idea as Bob and Clive. They were just going to drive around and see what they could see. But it also gave them an opportunity to talk.

The Major was having a little smoulder, so he wasn't very talkative. This didn't seem to worry Zelda at all, and she went into a torrent of words, which was normal for her – almost a stream of consciousness.

She shared her prolific internal dialogue as to where the elephant might actually be. There were all these different scenarios playing out in her head, and she just spoke them all out loud.

"The elephant may not be able to keep up with the man. Little Elsa may end up all lonely and looking for company. Perhaps she will find some cows and go and stand next to them. Perhaps she will go for a walk. Perhaps she will come back. Oh no, perhaps she will get lost and not know where she is. But if she goes on the jetty in the lake and it gives way under her and she falls in the water, I don't know that she can swim. What if she goes in the quarry? Will she be able to find her way out again? But if she is hungry, how will she find food to eat? Where will she sleep?" She turned to the Major at this point. She wanted to be sure that he was really getting the point. "Tell me we will get her back." She was working herself up to hysteria and just needed a reassuring word from him.

Major Askwith felt that she was missing the point that the elephant was not the main priority. So, rather stupidly, he felt the need to correct her. "We must not worry about the elephant. Finding the German is our first priority. Even if we see the elephant, we should carry on trying to find him.

Once we have him back, we can go and look for Elsa."

She put her foot on the brake abruptly. The truck screeched to a halt and the Major nearly banged his head on the windscreen. She rested her head on the steering wheel and started sobbing. She said repeatedly, "We must find her. We really must find her." She lifted her head and banged on the steering wheel.

Despite all his training, the Major was not very equipped to deal with a hysterical woman.

"There, there," he said pathetically. "But you must see my point. We must focus on the prisoner."

As far as she was concerned, they weren't going to go anywhere until they had resolved this matter. "No," she uttered. "We won't go anywhere until you agree with my point of view." She stared ahead with steely determination.

#

Tom and Jane set off on their bicycles together. Sneakily, they had been in the kitchen and made a sandwich and taken some fruit. It wasn't that they were planning a picnic, but they reckoned that they would be spending a long time hunting for the fugitives. The laird's estate was massive and interwoven with different paths and even roads in places.

No one in the mansion actually had a map of the estate in which they lived, which was ludicrous since they had been living there for quite a long time. All it would have taken was a trip to the library. That information was still held there, even in wartime, and could be released to a trustworthy source. Or a phone call to the owner would have sufficed.

They decided to start with the bits that they knew. On several earlier explorations, they had penetrated quite deeply into the estate, enjoying the mixture of woods and fields and even the occasional fishing lake. When they had time on their hands, it was a perfect way to spend an afternoon. Where they could, they rode side by side with each other and chatted. Some of the time this wasn't possible, and they had to go single file on the narrower paths.

"Tom, do you think we lead a charmed life here? Our surroundings are so beautiful, and we hardly notice them sometimes. If we don't fix this error, then we could be in deep trouble as a unit. Don't you think it's a bit like we've only been given one really important task to do since the unit was formed. I mean, I know we've got all these other mini projects on. But really, this was the only thing of any importance." She quietened down as she tried to navigate around some stones that were in her path and in danger of knocking her off the bike.

Tom had been level with her but now was going to have to go behind her as the path was going to narrow. She had come to a complete stop. Normally when they went cycling, she wore very practical clothes. Invariably, she would cycle in slacks.

Today, because of the haste in which they had left the house, she was wearing a skirt. It was windy and occasionally it was being blown around and he was getting an occasional glimpse of her thighs.

She turned to him and said, "You are being very quiet. Are you even paying any attention to what I'm saying?"

He knew her well enough to be partly truthful and so he said, "I am listening to you a little bit. I just got distracted by something." He thought it wise not to be specific about what was distracting him. He laughed inside and thought, "Well, I can't really say it's your milky thighs, woman. They are inflaming me!"

"Well, then say something, you muffin."

"I agree entirely. Somehow, we had better find both of them before it gets dark. And yes, we are blooming lucky. If we don't find them, our luck might run out and we'll be stationed somewhere else. My worst fear would be London. Even though my folks are there. Well, Jane, I want you to think like an elephant. You seem to get on well with her. Tell me where she would be going. I, for my part, will try and think like a German."

Jane replied, "Think like an elephant. You cheeky sod. What are you staring at anyway?"

As he was behind her, he couldn't possibly imagine why she should know that he was staring at her. Sometimes she seemed to have an uncanny level of knowledge about him that verged on the clairvoyant. She liked to say it was just because he was so transparent. He noticed that she had picked up speed and was cycling faster now. He was able to keep up, but only just. It often struck him how physically fit she was. Suddenly, she skidded to a stop.

As she spoke, she pointed at the bushes. "Look at those. They're all broken. It looks like something has crossed the path here." She left her bicycle on the ground. Tom propped his bike up against a tree.

"Do you think she has been through here?" Jane asked.

Having both dismounted from their bicycles, they pushed their way through the broken foliage.

Tom said, "I wouldn't be surprised if she has been through here. That looks suspiciously like an elephant dropping to me. What do you think?"

Jane picked up a stick and rolled it over. "Yes, Inspector Tom Hope, I think you're right."

They left their bikes and pushed further into the woods. The greenery was quite dense, so they were literally diving their way into it. They found more broken branches.

"Keep going. She has got to be here somewhere," Jane shouted as she went on ahead. And then, "I think I can see movement in front."

Tom was coming up closely behind her.

Suddenly, Jane broke into a run. He started to also. Together they burst into a clearing. There was a small lake, or what the Scottish would call a tarn, there. And lo and behold, there was Elsa. Her trunk was in the water, and she was sucking some up.

Jane tried to approach her gingerly, saying, "Come on, girl. Come on, girl. We want to look after you and help you."

Elsa turned and squirted water directly at the two of them. She then turned and headed off into the bushes.

Tom exclaimed, "The little blighter!" He and Jane were shaking water off themselves and doing their best to run at the same time.

As usual, Jane was more athletic than him as she ran ahead shouting, "Come on, Tom! We can't let her get away."

The chase continued through a couple of copses; they were discovering all sorts of nooks and crannies they did not know about. Eventually, Elsa slowed down to a walking pace and Tom and Jane were able to get nearer to her. This time, Jane decided not to say anything. Tom, on the other hand, was saying, "Come on, girl." She still had her collar around her neck. They were able to grab that and slowly, slowly they were able to bring her to a complete halt. They spent some time reassuring her and then they edged her round so that they could walk her back to the mansion. At this point, she seemed relatively happy and gave the occasional snort and little trumpet. When they had found her it had not occurred to either of them to look for the German. But they were reasonably sure that he was not in the vicinity; otherwise, they would have noticed something surely.

As they got near the mansion, she seemed to become a bit more reluctant and unwilling to move for a while. They coaxed her and got her on her way again. First of all, they headed to the room where the prisoner had been kept and where Elsa had been. But with the wall half broken, they decided that there was no point trying to put her back in. Under the circumstances, they decided that the trailer was a better choice. With a bit of manoeuvring, they got her up and back in. Tom went and found something to feed her.

For a few moments, they stood and watched her as she ate her food. To Tom's surprise, Jane put her arm out and over his shoulder. He felt good. He knew that Jane would probably just think she was being matey. He didn't look at her but enjoyed the warmth of the moment.

After five minutes she turned to him and said, "Come on, we'd better tell them we found her."

#

They were soon to discover that there was nobody to tell. Well, except for Ivan the Terrible. He seemed, however, to give off an air of being supremely indifferent to the whole affair. He just mumbled into his potatoes and spoke about how difficult it was to prepare a meal when he didn't know how many people were going to be there to eat it. He was not clairvoyant and how could they expect it. It was true, of course, because everyone was out looking and searching for the German and still under the impression that they also had to find the elephant.

Jane and Tom discussed whether or not it was going to be worth setting out and having a go at finding him themselves. They were still arguing about this – yes, having a proper argument – when the phone rang. Ivan was on the way to answer it. Jane saw what was happening and hastily made her way to overtake him en route to the telephone while still firing out angry words to her friend Tom, who was a bit stunned by the ferocity of the onslaught. They seldom reached this kind of impasse. Fortunately, the conflict was about to be broken by a higher force: Major Askwith.

He directed them to make haste to the village. A villager had told him that the prisoner had been seen making his way through it. Hoss had even been challenged. Unfortunately, it was by a woman in her 90s and she had not been able to give chase for obvious reasons. The Major said that the information was very reliable, though, and they needed to pursue it while it was still a warm lead. He said that he and Zelda would meet them near the church.

The Major was on the verge of concluding the call, but Jane managed to slow him down.

When she said, "We were able to find the

elephant," she heard a muffled squeal of delight. It was quite feminine and totally unlike the Major.

"Yes. Well, very well done. Thank you. Have you been able to secure her?" The muffled squeals were continuing in the background, but it was clear that the Major was trying to ignore them. He may even have been trying to suppress them.

"Thank you. Yes, we have been able to secure her. Although I'm not sure that's the right way of putting it. We have put her in her circus trailer for the moment." Jane then added, slightly pointedly, "Tell Zelda she seems perfectly happy. We have fed her, and she is okay for the moment."

The Major responded. He wasn't exactly cold, but he said in a distant voice, "Very well, then. Please get yourselves down here as quickly as you can. I appreciate that there are no vehicles and that you will have to cycle hard."

There had been no word from Clive and Bob. And Ivan did not know where Schmidt was.

Tom and Jane got ready as quickly as they could, then set off cycling to the village. They kept a good pace to begin with, until Jane's bike got a puncture on the front tyre. They lost a few minutes while they sorted this out. Fortunately, they had a puncture repair kit with them.

CHAPTER 14
THE PRISONER

Through fate or synchronicity, or whatever you might call it, Clive and Bob also ended up at the rendezvous. The truth be known, they were trying to head back to the mansion to have something to eat. They were driving through the village when they spotted Major Askwith at the side of the road and felt duty bound to stop – particularly as they were highly likely to be noticed as they were driving a huge army truck.

Clive and Bob got there about five minutes before Jane and Tom. So when Jane and Tom cycled up, it looked like they intended to be there.

The Major was striding around manfully while Zelda sat on the wall of the church and looked amused at his activity. She found it strangely appealing that he could be so serious about things. At times, she felt she held enough emotion in her body for both of them. It did her good to be under the influence of a man who was a lot calmer than she was. The Major looked at her and discovered that she was smiling at him. He assumed that he had her rapt attention and didn't realise that she was not, in fact, listening to a word he was saying.

Jane, Tom, Clive and Bob were actually listening. The Major was explaining that the old woman had seen the German go up the side of the church. He was proposing a pincer movement: one pair was go down the right-hand side of the church and another to the left. He pointed out that there was a footpath that diverged off and that another pair, in fact he and Zelda, would go down the footpath. He did his best to instil a degree of urgency in them. So, despite everyone being hungry, they had to ignore the fact that the pub was open and press forward. To be fair, everyone threw themselves into it. Even Zelda, once she had caught up with what was being discussed. She didn't need much of a briefing because when it came to it, all she had to do was tag along with the Major. They would not be far from each other, so if anybody did see Hoss, it should be possible to alert the others.

The sign for the footpath was at the church and it led off through the grounds. Once they were past the church, it wended its way through a dense wood and some fields which were between the two roads the other couples were tracking. The Major was moving forward quickly, and Zelda had trouble keeping up with him, which was surprising seeing as she was pretty fit... She didn't mind, but she was spending a long time looking at his back now. All of a sudden, they heard some whoops and cries coming from the field on their right-hand side.

The Major exclaimed, "Come on, Zelda. Somebody must have seen him." Then he added, "Look, there he is." They could see a figure dressed in grey clothes running through the field and Tom and Jane behind trying to catch up. They both tried to increase their pace so they could join in the chase. For some reason Tom and Jane were whooping regularly and making other loud noises. Maybe they were just enjoying it. It was, after all, a bit like playing fox and hounds or cops and robbers. Say what you like about the German, he could turn out a bit of speed when he chose to. Tom and Jane were just about keeping pace with him but were not catching up with him. The Major and Zelda were making progress towards the other runners but were still well behind.

Zelda spoke, "I think they're doing all that noise in order to try and attract Clive and Bob's attention." And she was right, as at that moment Clive and Bob appeared from the other side of the field and began to join in the chase. It was quite a funny sight. Maybe you should feel sorry for the prisoner as he was being strongly pursued and not only from one direction. To have three strands of pursuers closing in on you must feel a bit strange.

Hoss was feeling bewildered and trying to work out how to get away from his them. Just ahead of him he could see a railway line and to the other side a river. He was still on the path.

He had not left it because he thought if he was on grass and in bushes, he would make much slower progress and was more likely to be caught. He was feeling very breathless and was realising that he could not keep up this pace for much longer. Without too much thought, he decided to follow the railway line. It was a single track and he deduced from that that it was not a mainline and was probably a branch line or a freight line. To get onto the railway line, he had to slither down a bank. As he started to do this, he missed his footing slightly and rolled the rest of the way. When he reached the bottom, he did a half turn. As he looked up, he realised he was gazing into the eyes of a fox. He hoped the fox would run off, but instead the creature just stared at him. Maybe it could smell Elsa on him and was wondering why this human smelt like an elephant. It took a step towards him. It looked like it was going to sniff him and so Hoss waved his arms and said, "Verboten." The fox slowly turned its head and walked off nonchalantly. This tiny incident had slowed him down quite a lot and he realised that he needed to get to his feet and on his way again.

He stood up. He was feeling quite shaky. He started to run along the track bed, running who knows where, hoping that no train would come through. He tried to pace himself in such a way that his feet only touched the sleepers. To begin with, he was doing this to perfection. From the noise behind him, he knew that the six had got down the hill and were after him. He decided to try and take longer strides. This was where he went wrong because his foot missed the sleeper and landed on the ballast that was between the sleepers. He lost his footing completely and twisted his ankle. His body turned over and he lay with his nose next to the track.

He listened as they came nearer to him. At this juncture, he realised there was nothing else he could do other than admit defeat. He just lay there, ready for what came next. He wondered what their attitude would be; would they kick and beat him?

He could hear that they had slowed down their running. Obviously, they were well aware that he wasn't going to go anywhere fast now. He continued to gaze at the rail. Something in him, some stubbornness, prevented him from turning to face his captors.

Now he was aware that they were standing over him. It was the Major who was first to speak. He said in a quiet manner, "Well, you gave us a run for our money. I think we all got a bit of exercise today. Just keep calm while we take you back and bandage you." They improvised a stretcher using one of their coats and, with a bit of a struggle, got him up the bank and back to the village and then to the mansion.

CHAPTER 15
THE MANSION

Having arrived back at the mansion in the early evening, they took the prisoner into the dining room, lay him on the table and bandaged his leg. After they had done that, they sat him up and gave him a cup of tea to drink.

Bob and Clive were put in charge of him while the others went off to have a meeting. The question that the Major posed was what to do with the prisoner. The carpenter wouldn't be able to mend the room until the next day. It wouldn't make sense to put him in there overnight because he could easily escape again, although his mobility was now compromised.

They came up with two possible scenarios for keeping him secure. The first was that he could be kept on an upper floor in the mansion house. It was suggested that this could be the floor that the Major and Zelda were on. The other idea was to keep him in the circus trailer; of course, that would mean that he would be in with the elephant. He had already proved that he was compatible with her, so this would not be a risk to him.

Jane said, "I think he should be in the house. The trailer is much smaller than the room was. And it has been a stressful day for both the elephant and for the prisoner. It is only for one night and we can have a guard outside the room. I'm sure that we can also make it so the windows can't open."

The Major answered, "Well, I think he would be more secure in the circus trailer. I think that's what we should do with him. If he wanted to be more comfortable, he shouldn't have escaped in the first place. I think if we give him comfortable quarters then he may feel that he has won a victory by escaping."

Now that all this was agreed, they were ready to disperse. But as they started to leave the room, Schmidt said that he wanted to speak to the Major.

"I have the transcript of the prisoner's notes that he left in the notebook on the floor of the cell. I think it makes interesting reading. It is the most credible thing he has said so far. I would like you to read it and say whether you agree with me. I'm sure we can discuss it with him tomorrow and get some more detail."

The Major more or less snatched the transcript from him. The pressures of the day were getting to him. He said, "Let me see, then." Everyone else had gone. It was just him and Schmidt. He sat down and pulled out the paper. He read it again to himself slowly and carefully. As he did so, he became calmer. Slowly and deliberately, he spoke. "I see what you mean. This is a bit more hopeful. We may be finally getting somewhere with him. Yes, tomorrow we can go over this with him. I think I may sit in on it. Well, either myself or Jane. I still think we should stick him in the trailer, but maybe we could put a bed in with him. Then he doesn't have to sleep on the floor. As a little gesture of goodwill. I don't want him in the house. I just feel he will escape again." This last bit was a lie. He didn't want him in the house because he didn't want his time for activities with Zelda interfered with. This was not something that he would want to admit. In fact, if he thought about it more rationally, he would have realised that he was much too tired to be running around the corridor at night. But unfortunately, self-knowledge is not always a gift that we have.

#

Ivan the Terrible sent Bob around with the gong. The purpose was to announce that supper would be ready in 10 minutes. Schmidt looked at the Major and suggested that he let the prisoner join them for supper. If he ate alone, he would need to be supervised. His thought was that if the prisoner was sat in the midst of them all, he wouldn't be able to get away without them pouncing on him. Under the circumstances, it turned out to be a genius idea. We will get to that in a moment.

Everyone gathered in the dining room and

sat at the very table where they had bandaged the prisoner about an hour earlier. They squashed Hoss in between them all. He amused them by making the sign of the cross and saying grace before he started his meal. It was his first hot meal since he had come to the mansion. His fare previous to this had been fairly basic. The warmest thing he'd had was soup. The Major had told everyone not to talk about anything that might be considered to be covered by the Official Secrets Act. For obvious reasons, the prisoner should not be aware of anything that was going on. Of course, he was their biggest project, but there were other things that they were exploring, like exploding rats. This inevitably meant that the conversation was more domestic than normal.

 The Major was his normal taciturn himself. However, Zelda was sitting next to him and every now and then, when she thought nobody was aware, she would squeeze his knee or maybe even run her fingernail up his thigh. Of course, with all those people there, she didn't intend on doing anything, but she just enjoyed pushing his buttons. To her he was dark and mysterious and handsome and a pleasant alternative to all the superficial glitz of circus life.

 The conversation became animated and, of course, the other woman present at the meal was the culprit. Part of the reason Jane was so useful to the team was that she animated them. If she had not been part of the group, they would have been a very quiet bunch of people. Maybe the sort of people you could describe as dedicated or earnest. To be fair to Jane, she probably was not aware of the power she had over men. Tom was the one who lusted after her the most. She was, however, in everyone's thoughts at some point over the time that they were based at the mansion.

The conversation really got going when she turned to Tom and asked him whether he had ever read the book that he purchased on the way. If you remember, when he was looking at the wire rack, he was selecting which book to buy. On the train he had started reading *The Postman Always Rings Twice*.

He answered her, "I confess, I put it down on my bedside table that very evening and I haven't opened it since. Do you really think I should finish it? I suppose the reason I didn't pick it up again was I was thinking that you weren't doing anything other than trying to pick me up." He laughed. "For work reasons, of course."

"No. Out of the two books you were looking at, I genuinely thought that was the best one to read. It is quite absorbing. Pick it up again," she ordered him playfully.

Of course, all those seated around the table were listening to this with varying levels of attention. The prisoner seemed interested for some reason. He felt emboldened by the casualness of the meal and said, "We have that same book in Germany, you know: *Der Postbote klopft immer zweimal* by James Cain. It is a very good book."

Schmidt swore in German and then said, "I'm sure that can't be correct."

The prisoner was very even minded, so he swore back and then said, "Why? Do you think the Fuhrer thinks everything from America is bad? I'm sure I could put some records on my record player that you would recognise. But they would be by a German artist rather than an American."

Bob seemed to care about this subject, "You mean you knock off our best tunes?"

The prisoner seemed to realise that it would be stupid to give him a straight answer to that question. For a few moments, conversation round the table ceased. The Major gave Schmidt a gentle kick under the table. Schmidt knew exactly what this meant. The plan had been to relax the prisoner and make him say stuff that he wasn't expecting to say. So far, that wasn't succeeding. The weakness in their plan was that only Schmidt and the Major knew about it. They could have at least told a couple of the others, such as Jane and Tom. Schmidt decided to have a go at involving Jane by asking her a question.

"Is there a cinema near here? When did you last go and see a film?"

She straightened her back, tilted her head to one side and looked at him thoughtfully. "We should see if we could find a cinema near here. I do miss my weekly talking picture."

CHAPTER 16
AFTER HOURS

After a lengthy supper, a bottle of whiskey was produced from who knows where. Maybe somebody raided the laird's store; after all, his wine cellar was full of all sorts of famous label whiskies and wines. Those that wanted a dose of whiskey were allowed it. Amazingly, this included the prisoner Hoss, who eagerly volunteered his services to help drain the bottle. Nearly everyone stayed for a garrulous conversation. Zelda was the first to excuse herself. And then, after what seemed like 10 minutes, the Major also said that it was time for him to go and get some shuteye, as he put it. To some of those in the room, this will have seemed very transparent. The more generous spirited just thought, ah, well, they're both tired. And by anyone's standards, it had certainly been a long day.

Tom hung on for a bit then announced that it was time for him to go upstairs. Jane stood up and said that she would go as well. It is interesting that nobody thought for a minute that there was anything going on between the two of them. Mainly because patently there wasn't. And probably because they openly went round together for most of the time.

They said a few words to each other as they climbed the stairs, then Tom said goodnight to Jane and went up to the next floor. He went to his door and pushed it open. He stood at the entrance and gazed around the room and then went and washed his face.

He picked up his copy of *The Postman Always Rings Twice* and he stood at the window under the electric light and read a chapter which he had selected at random. It was quite simply written and quite absorbing. Then he was overcome by tiredness, and he tossed the book to one side.

He kind of threw himself on the bed, lay on his stomach and, because of his extreme tiredness, just fell asleep.

Possibly because of the alcohol, or maybe because of the sheer weight of the collective subconscious, he sank into a deep and vivid dream-filled sleep. The dream was about him and Jane. In the dream he was full of very clear, libidinous thoughts for her, imagining her body in all her curvaceousness and beauty, and what would happen if he had her. It was a strange dream and enabling in some ways.

In the dream, the same group of people had just had supper. The same conversations had gone on. Jane had queried why he had not read that book, *The Postman Always Rings Twice*. But in his dream, the question began to have a certain significance for him, as if it was some strange metaphysical question that he had to address. But the question wasn't about the meaning of the world. It was about whether or not he and Jane existed, whether they had any go in them as a couple. In the dream, he wondered whether she was using a code to signify that he should come and ring on her door. He spent a long time thinking about whether or not she was trying to drop a hint to him that if he came and rang on her doorbell that she would answer and let him in.

In the dream, he found another wing to the mansion and climbed the stairs to the corridor he knew would lead to Jane's room. When he got there, he stood and looked at the door for a few seconds, just wondering.

Now, in real life, there was not a bell on her door. In the dream, mysteriously he could see a large brass electric bell in the centre of her door. In his dream, this is what he actually did. He rang the bell twice. She opened it almost at once, as if she had been standing there waiting for him. He said nothing, but she gestured for him to come in. She was wearing her negligee, but he could quite easily imagine what was underneath because he could almost see the outline of her body. She drew him towards the bed.

Annoyingly, at this point in the dream he woke up. There was no climax to the scene. There was no conclusion that he could celebrate. He realised that he was still clothed and sat up on the bed. He could not work out what had woken him, but he was parched and maybe he needed a drink of water. Although there was a sink in his bedroom, it wasn't really the kind of water that you could drink. He was thirsty enough to leave the room and go and get a pint glass from the kitchen. Not wanting to take the glass back up to his room, he sat at the table, drank the water and thought.

He came to a conclusion in his head that Jane had been trying to give him a hint when she brought up that book. He began to read things into her actions. For example, they had walked up the stairs together. He started to think about the significance of ringing or knocking twice and decided that part of his problem was that he only ever used to knock once on the door of opportunity. Was the problem that he wasn't persistent enough with her?

It was this thinking that led him to her doorway. He got there, looked at it and, unlike the dream, there was no bell. The door was a different colour. It was magnolia and, for some reason, less welcoming. And, of course, he knew there was no bell. He put up his fist and knocked loudly on it twice. Fleetingly through his head came the thought that he was doing something extremely foolish. But he was too late.

He heard movement in the room. There was an interval before the door opened, and during that pause he thought to himself, "She is taking too long." The door opened slowly at first. But when she realised it was him, she opened it more fully. Her hair was dishevelled, and she was wearing very unglamorous pyjamas. It was clear that he had woken her from sleep.

"Tom, what on earth are you doing here?" she asked him.

"I am the postman ringing twice," he said, and at once felt foolish.

"It's 2:00 a.m. What are you talking about? The postman doesn't come at 2:00 a.m." She wasn't exactly irritated, but she seemed close to being it.

One of the other doors on the corridor opened, and she instinctively reached out and pulled him into the room. Her thinking was that she didn't want him to get into trouble, which was a slightly weird thought as they weren't at boarding school. But maybe in her head, trouble also constituted gossip.

Of course, Tom read something slightly different into her actions.

She pushed him into the armchair and said, "Sit still and talk to me."

He felt like he was on probation in some way. He had made his way into the holy of holies and everything depended on what he said next. He suddenly had the insight that he might still be drunk. This led him to the decision that he must be careful to speak clearly and slowly.

There was silence as he watched her wash

her face at the sink and then brush her hair as she looked into the mirror above the sink.

"Stay there," she said sternly. She climbed into bed and sat up, propped against the pillows. Her knees were raised as if she was going to read a book. "Now, tell me what all this nonsense is about you being the postman or something?" Then she joked, "I don't take deliveries in the middle of the night. Unless there is a very good reason." For obvious reasons, she didn't have a clue what had brought him to her door.

"I thought you were hinting." The fact that he was going to have to explain himself made him feel very foolish all of a sudden. He started to feel muddled in his head.

"How?" she asked. She sounded a bit like she was a queen demanding an explanation from a subject, but she was beginning to see the funny side.

"I thought you wanted me to knock twice. Like the postman," he said, and then felt extremely foolish.

She got it now, "Oh, the postman always knocks twice!" She started laughing, and then it dissolved into giggling. "You really are the biggest idiot sometimes, Tom. Go on, explain a bit more. What on earth did you think I was on about?" She tried to stop laughing, straightening the coverlet and trying to look as if she was going to pay attention and be serious.

Tom made a ham-fisted attempt at

explaining exactly what had happened, about the dream and about how he had gone to the kitchen and thought things. And then thinking those things, he had concluded that he should come upstairs and knock on her door. She was just beaming at him. She didn't seem to mind, but it was clear that sex wasn't going to happen. It wasn't necessary for her to say anything about it. He could just tell from the way she was talking to him. He felt doomed to live forever in the friendship zone.

She looked at him and she knew that she liked Tom, but the war had somehow messed up her thinking about romantic relationships. She had never told Tom that she had been engaged to somebody who was killed in France. It had made her very cautious about forming emotional attachments to men. Her fiancé, who had been killed, had been someone who she had hoped to have children with.

Tom was still having an attack of obedience. In his soporific state, he was content to watch her until she was willing to talk to him again. It would not be too long before she opened her mouth again because she did like to contribute.

Then she said, "You really are a bit mad, Tom, aren't you? First of all, the title of that book is *The Postman Always Rings Twice*. That's 'rings', Tom, not 'knocks'."

He kind of stuttered, "Well, yes, I know, really. Well, I think I know. Oh, I don't know. Ring or knock? What's the difference? In the dream, it seemed to be about knocking on the door of opportunity. Although I do recognise that it was a big doorbell on your door. In the dream," he added, as if he thought she couldn't follow.

Now she was laughing at him more openly. She really didn't know what to say to him at that moment because she didn't want to disappoint him. However, for the time being he was on a hiding to nothing. There was an absence of wanting on her part and it is very difficult to explain that to a man sometimes. It wasn't even like he had competition, though.

"Tom can't we..." she trailed off as Tom clapped his hands to his head and said, "Oh no." He sank further back into his chair.

"You don't know what I was going to say."

"Yes, I do. You are going to say, 'Can't we be friends?'" He sighed resignedly as he said it.

She looked a bit more serious now and said, "That isn't exactly what I was going to say. Tom, can't we wait a while? I do like you, I just think it might need to be at a future time, that is all. I do have my reasons. It's not just me being whimsical."

"How long do you need?" He was thinking if it was just a couple of weeks or a month, he could probably manage that.

She didn't like to tell him that she didn't know how long it would be. After all, it could be never. For the moment, she preferred to dodge the question. "Tom, it is very late. I think you should go back to your bedroom. Let's do something tomorrow evening. Go to the cinema or something." She got out of bed, perhaps realising that she was going to have to shepherd him out of the room. He gradually rose to his feet and headed towards the door. As he opened the door, he looked back at her, and she kissed him on the cheek.

"No hard feelings?" she asked.

"No, nothing hard at all." His feeble joke over, he tried to be more serious. "I don't think I will lose interest."

CHAPTER 17
HOSS

The prisoner had also gone to bed drunk. Since his captivity, he had become totally unused to alcohol. He was bemused at the way his captors had treated him last night. He had expected to be in solitary confinement following his recapture. That would have been the most logical outcome.

And my God, these English people were eccentric in the way they kept you prisoner. He had been expecting to be back in the large white room. It couldn't be that difficult to mend it, for heaven's sake. He wasn't sure whether to be amused or outraged because he found himself in the circus trailer with that sweet little elephant. He just couldn't understand the English captors' fetish for putting him in a room with an elephant. And then they would childishly pretend that it hadn't happened by refusing to discuss it.

There is no doubt that Elsa was pleased to see him again. As soon as he had been led up the ramp and the iron gate was fastened, she had slowly sauntered across to him. She offered her head for a scratch. He no longer felt any sense of danger when he was with her. Once again, he found himself crooning to her, sometimes lullabies and sometimes just German wartime songs. Nothing patriotic but dance songs from the clubs. Elsa really liked his singing. He tried doing a one-legged dance. It was a surprise to him when she also raised one leg. Maybe this was how Zelda taught her tricks. In a relaxed way, and not at all systematically, they had a little drunken dance around the trailer. Well, of course Elsa wasn't drunk. They hadn't put anything in her water. She was a good girl.

He found himself confessing to her. He said, "Elsa, I really miss my wife and my children. I think I have been extremely stupid. I should have kept my mouth shut when I was near Hitler and his gang. Then I wouldn't have had to flee." He wasn't blind drunk or stupidly drunk, but he was intoxicated. In vino veritas. He just spoke the truth to her. It was good for him that there was nobody hiding near the trailer listening. Because if they had been, they would have heard all his true intentions. If they had, what would happen next? Nobody had mentioned his confession, for example. He assumed that Schmidt, or maybe the Major, had found it by now. They had said that the room wouldn't be mended until tomorrow, and they were almost apologetic at putting him in the circus trailer. He laughed to himself because he imagined there must have been another cell available somewhere. But maybe not. He thought to himself how the English are like frog spawn. You can look at them and think that you can see clearly what's inside them, but when you try and put your finger on it, it's all slippery and slides out of the way. He laughed to himself and lay on the floor and said, "English frog spawn, slippery, slippery, slippery." Elsa stood above him and put her trunk out as if she was trying to tickle his tummy. He realised he was just lying on hay. He saw that there was a blanket next to him and reached out and pulled it towards him and tried to make a little nest for himself. Elsa lowered herself and lay next to him. He listened to the rhythm of her breathing as he fell asleep. She didn't fall asleep at once herself, and she was hoping that he was going to talk to her in German again. After all, it was so wonderful that he knew that language. A little tear welled up in her eye. He didn't see that, that was just her little secret. A tear for Germany and all that it had become. She, of course, was an elephant. She didn't know what was really happening. She just knew that she was in a different country now.

#

The next morning, at about ten, two guards came for him and took him to his big white room. Both wondered why they didn't just leave him in the trailer.

He thought he was going to be interrogated again. He was led into the room and seated behind the table. Instead of there being just two interrogators, there were three: the Major, Schmidt and Jane were sitting opposite him and looking strangely expectant. He was feeling mischievous and didn't know whether he was going to cooperate with them. He decided to talk about the elephant.

"When will you bring my darling little friend the elephant over to keep me company?"

The Major coughed and said, "We can't talk about that now." If it had been Jane or Schmidt opening the encounter, they probably would have caved and talked about Elsa. The Major was a great one for believing that a rule was a rule.

Hoss was not to be deterred. "I think you should bring her over soon. I'm missing her. She helps me to feel looked after." Now, really, in his heart he knew he was being stupid. Fortunately, their agenda was not what he thought it was.

"The three of us have read your confession. We are prepared to believe that you are who you say you are. If you take us to where you hid the papers, we can arrange for you to be sent to an internment camp for the rest of the war. We will even try to arrange preferential treatment for you. Of course, we won't be able to get your wife and kids over here, but at least at the end of the war, you might be able to be reunited with them, God willing. If we take you back to where you brought the plane down, do you think you can take us to where you hid the papers? We want them."

When the Major said all this to him, he felt

strange. He should have felt relieved because it was what he wanted. He had geared himself up to the thought that he was going to be punished. Instead, they seemed to be on the verge of overlooking what he had done the previous day. It was even as though they didn't see him as one of the enemy. He said, "I'm pretty sure that I can find it again if you take me."

They only spoke to him for about 15 minutes. It was agreed that they would all go for a little drive the following day. They had the exact coordinates of where he had been picked up. The Major hadn't asked permission from anyone to do this. But it seemed the best thing in the circumstances. The Cabinet Office still had not been notified about the prisoner's escape. It would be like the incident hadn't happened. The official record would just look like they didn't bother interrogating him the previous day. His interrogators behaved like they had everything they needed now and left him in peace. The table was removed from the room. He just had his blanket on the floor to lie on.

After about two hours, he got up and started banging on the door. The guards opened it and stood there, surprised. He had a very simple request: "Can you put me in the circus trailer, please? I'm missing the elephant."

CHAPTER 18
THE ROAD TO FRASERBURGH

The following morning, all were up early. There was a communal sense of purpose amongst everyone that wasn't often visible. It had been decided that they were going to take two vehicles. For purely practical reasons, the prisoner was to be taken in the truck as it was possible to seat three people in the front. Hoss was to sit in the middle; he would be handcuffed and attached to an anchor point which was near the gear stick. Jane was to drive and Tom was to sit next to the prisoner.

The Major and Schmidt would convoy with them in the staff car. Zelda had wanted to come as well, but Major Askwith put his foot down. He said brusquely that this was official business, and she was not to attend. He would pay for his casual remark by having favours withdrawn for at least the night. Fortunately for him, she was always quick to forgive.

They had released the prisoner from the circus trailer at 8:00 a.m. He had been allowed to have breakfast with them. Then, after a few moments attending to what was necessary, they left. The journey was close to 100 miles and a lot of it was on minor roads. Navigation during the war was always much more of an effort because many of the road signs were taken down.

There was not much to note about the journey other than the fact that Hoss had a little outburst. They had got as far as Buckie when it happened. It seems that he had been bottling something up for some time – namely a feeling he had that Jane was being too personal when she was changing gear. She was focused on the driving and oblivious of the fact that every time she changed gear, the gear stick and her hand brushed against Hoss. He had an almost puritanical sense of propriety. So, a good part of the journey had involved him secretly cringing at being touched by a woman other than his wife. Finally, he could bear it no more and interjected.

"Stop stroking my thigh, woman!" he exclaimed.

Jane put the brakes on and stared at him. "Don't call me 'woman'!"

The two of them glared at each other. Then Jane asked, "What exactly is your problem?"

"You were brushing me with your hand. It is too personal, and I don't like it."

"Show me," she said impatiently.

"How can I? I'm not the one changing gear."

She started the engine up again and drove slowly for a quarter of a mile. She was angry to begin with and her driving was very jerky. Then she pulled over to the side of the road. Reluctantly, she found herself aware that Hoss was right but found that she was simmering with indignation – because why would it be so dreadful to be touched by her anyway?

"Tom." She chose to address him rather than Hoss. "Can you take the handcuff off its current position and put it somewhere else?"

Tom had kept silent so far throughout the whole exchange. The only solution he could come up with was actually less comfortable for Hoss, but he was too proud to admit it.

The rest of the journey went without incident. Around midday, they reached their destination. The German had landed his plane near Fraserburgh, although he had missed the airfield there by about a quarter of a mile and had flown into a haystack. Most of the remnants of the crash had been removed, but he was able to show them some of the wreckage. They walked around for a while. He said that he was trying to get his bearings.

"There. You see that church over there? Let's walk towards that." He was handcuffed to Tom and trying to walk briskly. Tom yanked back the handcuff a bit and said, "Slower."

All of them, Including the Major and Schmidt, moved off towards the churchyard. The prisoner slowly led them around to the other side of the church. Then he pointed, "Round the back of that shed there." It looked like a gravedigger's shed or maybe one for the groundsman of the church. The door was padlocked.

"Don't worry about that," the prisoner said. He got down on his hands and knees. He put his hand under the door and around to the right. The door was so ill-fitting that it was easy to do this without ever opening it. He pulled out a canvas bag which he then proffered to the Major. "Here you are. This is what you want."

The Major walked over to the church porch. Everybody followed. He knelt down on the tiled floor in the porch and tipped the contents of the bag out in front of him. It was an unusual collection of things. A pile of minutely shredded paper and mouse droppings. A tin with German writing on that proved to contain a collection of photographs of the prisoner's family. A pipe and a compass. That was it. The Major sifted through the paper. Most of the fragments were far too tiny to even see what the words said on them, but it was possible to discern that there had been writing. There were a couple of larger fragments that had a bit of a crest from a German document on. The Major stood up and ordered Schmidt to "clean that mess up". He went and stood in the churchyard and just gazed into the distance.

Hoss was still kneeling where the contents of the bag had been tipped out. He was speaking in German, maybe praying or even swearing.

#

The next morning, they had a meeting to review

the project. A further report was due back to the Cabinet Office and this had been delayed because of the escape of the prisoner. The Major discussed with all who were present how to present the information. He was really quite candid when he was talking to all those gathered and said that he thought the thing was a complete failure. One or two people spoke up and said they thought maybe he was being too bleak in his assessment. After all, the elephant had brought about some sort of result, even though it wasn't the expected one.

Schmidt said, "I really think we should try and present this as a success. The biggest problem, of course, is that the outcome is not good. In a sense, that is just fate, though. I mean, who could expect that a mouse, or even a party of mice, would eat the documents? We aren't responsible if the German hid the things in a stupid place."

"I'm sorry if you are perturbed at my opinions. Of course, we have to make it look like it's a success. Needless to say, I was never going to admit to the Cabinet Office that it was a failure, but I feel that I need help in presenting the information in the best possible way. In the military life, one should never admit defeat. Or certainly never call it defeat, even though everyone knows it is," the Major answered.

Tom spoke up. "Well, I think we can say things like we have learned valuable lessons. If the Cabinet Office still don't know that the elephant and the prisoner escaped, do we need to tell them? Obviously, we shouldn't try reconstructing the documents from the tiny pieces. I doubt that would even be possible." He tailed off.

The discussion continued for a while, but they were in want of a conclusion.

Eventually, the major tried to bring things to a close by saying, "I will just do a brief report and be as bland as possible. I will try to underplay the failures but will admit to them. Yes, we produced some sort of result. Of course, putting the prisoner with the elephant made something happen, but it wasn't what we were expecting at all. Although I suppose we got as far as a confession. I will, however, recommend to the Cabinet Office that we have no more experiments like this." And with that, he left the matter for the evening. The team did not see the report that he eventually sent.

CHAPTER 19
TWILIGHT

This is the nurse's nephew Sam here. She has asked me to supply the final two chapters. If the truth be told, Tom has not been very well at all. I'm sitting beside him at the hospice. So, as he has just pointed out, he is still the artistic director for this project. As you can probably tell from that, although he is weak, he is still strong-willed. As proof of this, he has asked me to write this as if he was writing it for the book. If you took out this paragraph, it would be his story all along.

We come into this world naked, and a lot of our last days are spent semi-naked with a nurse washing us. In other words, you might say we go from dependence to a final state of having every need looked after by a dedicated team. Of course, not everyone's life is like this, and as we saw during the war, some people die prematurely. Still, this isn't a book about philosophy. It's just an untold story from the war that might tickle your fancy. The English readers will understand what that means, but the American ones might think it means something completely different.

Tom's stay in the hospice was a bit longer than expected. It might be because of his own will, or it might be because the nurse suggested this project to him. Once he got started on it, he really wanted to finish it. There are some loose ends to tie up, of course. Aren't there always?

He stayed with the SOE until the end of the war. Most of their later activities were less crazy than the one he was involved in first. They always tried to be inventive, though. He stayed there because of the injury to his legs meant that he couldn't really serve anywhere else in the military. That said, the impediment got milder and milder as time went on.

Things with Jane never really took off. Well, not in a romantic sense anyway. They were probably about the closest friends that they could ever be. She trusted him in a way that she didn't trust other people.

As was the way with a lot of people during the war, their friendship got interrupted. They got separated by the fact that she took up an alternative posting with SOE that meant she had to work in France. She died in France in 1944. Tom didn't know a lot of detail, although it appears that she died at the hands of the Gestapo. Once she left Scotland she always kept in touch, and they would write to each other regularly. It could be a bit mysterious as neither could actually mention what they were working on, so they would resort to telling each other anecdotes about the people in the nearby village or people they had met. They did manage to have a couple of face-to-face meetings, though. The last time he saw her she seemed very troubled, but she said that she couldn't talk about it. He felt that he wanted to comfort her, but that was not possible. They did, however, spend a long time sitting next to each other on the sofa in the lounge of the Edinburgh hotel they were staying in, quietly drinking more and more and talking about their plans for the future. The war would end one day, and then, of course, they would be free to make plans. They both loved Scotland and thought it would be nice to live near each other.

Jane made a point of saying something that only made sense afterwards. She turned to him and said, "Promise me you will not do anything foolish like wait for me. I feel you have been waiting for me for a long time." She was holding his hand now and continued, "This is the sort of war where what will be will be and what won't be won't be. I'm terribly sorry but I just can't be relied upon. Not in the same way that a lot of women can be." His instinct was that she wanted to say a whole lot more but something was preventing her – most likely the consequences of sharing information in a public place.

The gaps between letters became longer. He knew that it was outside her control but would still expectantly check the post each day.

One day in May 1944, the Major called him to his office.

"I'm very sorry that there is some bad news for us all, but especially for you."

Tom, who had been standing, sat down heavily on the chair. He braced himself because he knew what Major Askwith was going to say next. He wanted to cry and shout but didn't feel that he could. In the event, he just said, "I see."

The Major said, "She will be sorely missed." He looked at Tom and added, "You stay here, and I will go and tell the others." He was, after all, quite a good judge of character.

Once he was alone, Tom broke down.

CHAPTER 20
THE VISITOR

For a few days, Tom had been hovering between life and death. It was as though he had some unfinished business that needed to be done before he could go in peace. His nurse, the 'nurse with no name', and her nephew Sam took a lot of interest in him. You aren't supposed to have favourites as a nurse, but it is true to say that sometimes one patient stands out more than others. When she had suggested the project, she hadn't imagined that it would take so much of his time up or that he would become so preoccupied with it. She wondered whether that was because it was a story that had to be told. It gave him something to concentrate on in his last days. She could tell that he was most energised on the days that he had done a good storytelling.

When they weren't at the hospice, she sometimes discussed with Sam whether there was any truth to the story. Sam had a tendency to just shrug and say, "Does it matter?" One time, she said, "I hate to think that he is just fooling himself."

"Now, come on, Aunty. You can't complain –

you wanted him to do it, to keep himself occupied."

"I know," she said. But she gazed thoughtfully into the middle distance, and Sam knew that she really wanted more.

A week later, when she wasn't on duty, somebody phoned the hospice. A young woman. She asked if she could come and see Tom. She said that she was phoning first because she had to travel down from Argyll and wanted to be sure it was possible to see him. The hospice manager was a bit cautious at first because the woman openly declared she was not a relative. Normally speaking, in the last days it's only relatives or close friends who get to see patients. Tom was in the difficult position of not really having anyone to visit him. As he had kind of been starved of visitors, the hospice manager decided she would say yes, but she did warn the caller that Tom might not be alive by the time she got there.

The next day, the young woman presented herself at the hospice reception.

"I have come to see Tom Hope." She identified herself as the woman who had phoned previously.

"Tom is quite poorly today. If you bear with us, we will just make him comfortable."

#

Tom had been asleep most of the morning. He was surprised when the nurse came in and decided to prop him up. She fluffed up all his pillows and rested him against them and even washed his face.

He decided to summon up some energy for human interaction.

"What's got into you today?" he asked her.

"You have a visitor. You'd better be on your best behaviour. No swearing now."

"You must be mistaken. They must be for somebody else." Then, as a joke, he added, "I hope it's not the vicar."

"It's certainly not a vicar, and I don't think he's going to try again after the last time."

The nurse finished straightening everything up, and then she turned to him and said, "I think you're shipshape now."

There was a pause. And then, gingerly, a woman of about 30 pushed the door open.

"Tom? Are you Tom Hope?" she asked.

"Yes, I am."

He looked at her with interest. He shifted position and waited until she got a bit nearer.

"Do take a seat," he said. "Jane, how did you find me?" He felt sure that his brain must be misfiling information. This couldn't possibly be Jane. Jane was dead. But this young woman was so like her.

The woman spoke softly to him. "I'm Jessica. I'm not Jane."

"Are you sure?" He put his hand out to touch hers. "You look like my friend Jane." He was fighting back tears.

Jessica let him hold her hand. She could see that he was trying to compose himself.

He rang the bell for the nurse. "Please could we have tea and biscuits for my visitor?"

He could not help himself, he was staring at her. He felt he should explain himself, so he said, "You remind me of someone I once knew. But you say you're not Jane. Should I remember where I met you?"

He released her hand and she sat back in her chair. She was smiling gently at him. She started to speak. "I really should explain myself. I found that you were here…" The door opened. The nurse came in.

Jessica said, "I have been told that I mustn't tire you out, and see, they have already sent somebody to check up on me." She turned to smile at the nurse.

"Tom, I just came to see that you had everything."

"Yes, all is well. Thank you."

"I will leave you to your visitor. If you get into any discomfort, press the buzzer to let me know."

"Jessica, you were going to explain where I knew you from?"

"Well, Tom. I feel a bit foolish now I'm here. You don't actually know me at all. The reason you feel that you might recognise me is because I'm related to Jane. My mother is her younger sister."

He tried to sit up and look at her more closely. She instinctively leant towards him a bit as though she recognised his need to try and verify what she was saying.

"Yes, I can see that you are like her. It is nice to meet you, Jessica, but I'm not quite sure why you are here."

"My mum moved house recently and before she moved, we had to go through a whole load of papers. You know what it's like when people are trying to shed some of their stuff in order to move into a smaller place. Well, we came across something that we didn't jettison. But we held on until after the house move. It was a small brown suitcase, one of those that must have been from the war. My mum told me she had never really been through it because it had been so difficult for her emotionally. The suitcase contained everything that was returned by the War Office when my Aunt Jane died in the war. There were one or two of her possessions, things like a headscarf and a hairbrush, as well as lots of letters and her diaries and some photographs."

Tom was listening, but he didn't say anything.

"So," she continued, "we read all of her diaries, we looked at all the photos and we read all the letters. Most of them were from you, Tom." She started to feel self-conscious, as if she must excuse herself. "Listen, I'm sorry, Tom, this might be a bit overwhelming for you. If you need me to go, just say."

He smiled and said, "No, do continue." He didn't tell her how weak he was feeling. He didn't want to stop now that she had started telling him.

"Well, Mum and I both began to think that we should really try to contact you, just to show you some of the photographs and a couple of the letters. There is one in particular that we felt you should see because you probably never saw it. If you're feeling tired, I could show you some photographs first. Then I could either read the letters to you, or you could get the nurse to read them to you after I go."

She started to show him some photographs. He told Jessica that he remembered now that Jane did have a small camera that she used. One of those little Kodak ones with roll film. He used to tease her as she was forever taking photographs. He used to say that somebody would one day "mistake her for a spy". As soon as he said that, the enormity of it hit. Tears welled up in his eyes and he went silent for a bit.

"I am tiring you."

"Only a little. And I don't want you to go."

Jessica looked at him, and she thought she shouldn't stay much longer.

"Tell you what, I'll just read you a couple of things from her diary. There is a letter too, but I will leave that with you. It's addressed to you, anyway. I apologise. We have read it but of course we didn't know at the time that it was for you. I think the only competition you had for her affections was the elephant. A lot of the diary was redacted before it was returned to the family. It was quite hard for us to get a clear idea of what on earth the two of you were doing with an elephant. It seemed to occupy you. I suppose we'll never know."

Jessica read to him four or five days' worth of diary entries that hadn't been redacted. Maybe they had been left because the censor just thought that Jane had an interest in elephants. Included in what she read was the incident where Tom visited her in the middle of the night.

He couldn't help this, as a side effect of the illness, but as he was being read to, his eyes slowly kept closing. He would fight to open them again. Sometimes he would make himself say things like, "Continue."

"That's enough for today, Tom." She closed the diary and gathered her things together. She left by his bed some of the photographs and a letter in an envelope. It was self-explanatory. She wouldn't need to wake him to tell him.

She leant forward, kissed him on the forehead and left the room.

#

Tom woke up a couple of hours later. When he first did so, he began to ask himself whether he had dreamt the whole affair. Dreamt that this young woman had been to see him. He looked at his watch and saw that it was another hour before supper. He contemplated going back to sleep, but then decided that he would sit up. He looked over to his left, where his water could usually be found on the bedside table. There were some photographs there and a letter. One of the photographs was of him and Jane standing next to the elephant. He guessed that Schmidt must have taken it. Or maybe Bob. Both Jane and Tom had big smiles on their faces. It looked like they had just finished laughing about something. He put the photographs down and started to read the letter. It was from Jane and addressed to him. He began to see now why Jessica had made this special trip. There was a custom during the war that if you were going on a perilous mission that you would write a letter which was to be opened in the event of your death. The letter was definitely addressed to him; however, it was one of those types of letters. It was a love letter. She said that she had had time to reflect before travelling and she wanted him to know and be sure about certain things and also about the strength of her feelings for him.

He cried gently, and let the letter fall onto the coverlet of the bed. After a few minutes, his eyes closed and gradually his breathing became shallower. He slipped from life.

BOOKS BY THIS AUTHOR

Spindrift

Breakfast At Brewer Street

Truth: A Modern Fantasy

Printed by Amazon Italia Logistica S.r.l.
Torrazza Piemonte (TO), Italy